PRAISE FOR *CHANGING STORIES*

"Jairo de Oliveira is an advocate for refugees and builds a compelling, convicting case for every Christian to do the same. He masterfully sketches a rich biblical narrative of compassion for the forcibly displaced. God's heart for refugees is undeniable and de Oliveira has built a bridge for us from inertia to engagement, helplessness to hope. He invites us to cross it with him and share Christ with the nations in our own backyards."

—Audrey Frank, author of *Covered Glory:*
The Face of Honor and Shame in the Muslim World

"Jairo provides a fresh, biblical approach to a subject that has waned in the media but has only increased on the world stage. Stories like those of Aisha, Rashida, and Samira reduce the world stage to a microcosm enabling the reader to see the true faces of refugees and prompting a rise to an action for the sake of fellow image-bearers. He demonstrates how even a small church in Columbia, South Carolina, can have a global impact and provides practical tools to enable any church to join the Lord in caring for the most persecuted and desperate people on earth."

—Alex Pettett, Executive Director of World Witness, the foreign mission agency of the Associate Reformed Presbyterian Church

"In addition to providing a solid biblical and theoretical foundation to the topic of refugees, Jairo's research is also told through his own lens: as an immigrant embedded with immigrants. His humble and loving approach will give readers practical tips and thought-provoking conversations to consider as they respond to the current refugee phenomenon."

—Brian Hébert, Associate Professor of Intercultural Studies, Fuller Seminary Texas, and Co-founder and Director of Training and Strategy, Urban Catalyst

"Migration has been present through the long human journey over the centuries. Famine, wars, poverty, naturals disasters, and injustice have forcibly moved entire families and nations from one place to another over the centuries. Today, we witness one of the most significant movements of displaced people and refugees in human history. Nearly 80 million people have had to move out of their hometowns towards the four corners of the world. What a moment in history! Jairo de Oliveira has written an invaluable contribution to the missionary movement, to the ones in the historical sending countries—mainly from the Anglo-Saxon world—and to the newly Global South missionary movement. His research embraced deep biblical and sociological perspectives about the challenge of the diaspora and the refugee service, with a special mention to his thoughtful reflections on best practices and field evaluation in the refugee work. A brilliant contribution!"

—Allan E. Matamoros, Director for Middle East and North Africa, Partners International, Field Director, COMIBAM International, Vision 5:9 Chairman of the Steering Committee

"How do we think biblically and act practically regarding the current global refugee crisis? In *Changing Stories*, Jairo de Oliveira, an experienced global Christian worker, tackles both of these questions and offers a valuable resource to churches questioning their part in ministering to refugees. Pastors, seminary students, and all Christian believers will benefit from this book."

—Edward L. Smither, Dean and Professor of the College of Intercultural Studies, Columbia International University, and President of the Evangelical Missiological Society

"In *Changing Stories*, Jairo de Oliveira invites us to think biblically about the refugees of the world facing a humanitarian crisis and living under pressures of uncertainty. Each refugee represents a human being created in God's image that the Almighty is bringing close to us. The author also reminds us of the opportunity to serve them in love, kindness, and compassion. Indeed, the global church will be blessed with this precious and relevant book."

—Jeferson F. Chagas, Founder and President, Hikmah International Ministries

"*Changing Stories* captures the heart of the issue of one of today's greatest opportunities facing the church—people on the move. Jairo reminds us that at the center of the mass migration of people are individuals, each one loved by their Creator. Framed in a biblical imperative to 'treat the alien and stranger among us as one of our native-born' (Lev 19:34), Jairo offers practical tools by way of questions and case studies to help the believer respond with compassion and friendship."

—John Becker, Global Strategy Director, AIM International, and Co-founder of Greater Nuba Action Coalition and Diaspora Peoples in Europe Network

"God's people are pilgrims. Our homeland is heaven. Millions of refugees are on a pilgrimage today, searching for a new life. It makes sense for us, as God's people, to be the ones with open arms to welcome them. *Changing Stories* is a reflection that arises from praxis. Jairo de Oliveira, a Brazilian pilgrim, with his community of faith in the USA, teaches us how to love the foreigner. I recommend the book as well as the author. As a brother in Christ and as a friend, I have followed Jairo closely since his first years of ministry in Africa. He stands out for combining a love for Christ and people with remarkable zeal and academic excellence."

—José Roberto Prado, Founder and CEO of ABUNA, and Brazilian National Facilitator, Refugee Highway Partnership

"At a time when more people have been forcibly displaced than at any time in recorded history, many Christians are unsure of how—or if—to respond. In *Changing Stories*, Jairo de Oliveira draws on Scripture, meticulous research, and his many years of experience in refugee ministry to make the case that God is at work amid the global refugee crisis. Practical and persuasive, I strongly recommend it."

—Matthew Soerens, US Director of Church Mobilization, World Relief, and National Coordinator, Evangelical Immigration Table

"This book tells us of a Brazilian PhD student, speaking Arabic to serve Syrian refugees in South Carolina. Reread that sentence and consider it for a moment. I'm humbled to learn from Jairo that Americans need not be afraid of refugees to our country because of the stringent precautions that our government requires two years of screening before they're allowed to arrive. He bears the stories of his experiences with the fresh perspective of being a foreigner and traveler himself—able to empathize with these new Americans in ways that we need to hear."

—Nate Scholz, Medina Focus Coordinator,
Refugee Highway Partnership

"This book will help refugee ministries to consider the strategic impact of their work. As a participant of the workgroup that created the original *Best Practices for Refugee Ministry* with Refugee Highway Partnership, this is the first book that I am aware of to include a description of these practices in action. It gives a first-hand example of the usefulness of these principles. More ministries should do the hard work of applying and evaluating their ministry practices among refugees."

—Paul Sydnor, Europe Regional Leader, International Association for Refugees, Global Diaspora Network of the Lausanne Movement

"When confronted with the immense scope of the current migration crisis, it is easy to become overwhelmed and hopeless. *Changing Stories* provides a fresh vision and deeper motivation for Christians to become personally involved in the lives and stories of the refugees that God has placed around us. This book reminds us that our response to this crisis depends not only on Christian compassion but also on obedience to God's commands. In addition, by sharing the personal stories of refugees and those who welcome them, Jairo shows how this feeling of hopelessness can be turned to joy in seeing God write a new chapter in the lives of both refugees and volunteers. We have been blessed to see the way that God has used Jairo and his family in the lives of refugees here in Columbia, South Carolina, and we look forward to seeing how God will use this practical and timely book to spur on his church!"

—Robert Turner, Pastor, Arsenal Hill Presbyterian Church

"There is plenty of information about refugees today. There are stats, graphs, maps, and charts. As important as those are, stories capture the true essence of what is happening as people are on the move globally. Jairo de Oliveira writes about these stories and reminds us of the humanity amidst the overwhelming numbers."

—Ted Esler, Former Executive Vice President, Pioneers USA, and President, Missio Nexus

"Jairo de Oliveira has complemented his years of personal refugee ministry experience with in-depth research to produce a timely resource intended to help local churches engage in effective ministry among forcibly displaced people. Jairo offers many specific insights concerning how to come alongside Muslim refugees in ways that demonstrate respect and love in action. Jairo's use of the *Best Practices for Refugee Ministry* document of the Refugee Highway Partnership is a helpful example of applying this ministry assessment tool in a specific refugee ministry context. The book will be particularly helpful to churches in the United States and Europe."

—Tom Albinson, Founder and President, International Association for Refugees, and Ambassador for Refugees, Displaced, and Stateless People, World Evangelical Alliance

"Displacement and homelessness are profound and disturbing realities today. Jairo de Oliveira invites us to engage these realities with love, compassion, and integrity. The missiology behind *Changing Stories* demonstrates that God is already there, amid the pain and suffering. Moreover, he is inviting us to be part of his redemptive presence, healing touch, and reconciling arms. This book is a sign of hope for this troubled time and will encourage and challenge us to engage these realities from our own vulnerabilities, a context where God's grace finds home. It is a privilege for me to celebrate and recommend this account of hope and transformation."

—Zazá Lima, Executive Director of Pueblos Musulmanes Internacional (PMI)

Changing Stories

Changing Stories

Responding to the Refugee Crisis
Based on Biblical Theory and Practice

JAIRO DE OLIVEIRA

Foreword by J. D. Payne

WIPF & STOCK · Eugene, Oregon

CHANGING STORIES
Responding to the Refugee Crisis Based on Biblical Theory and Practice

Wipf & Stock
An Imprint of Wipf and Stock Publishers
199 W. 8th Ave., Suite 3
Eugene, OR 97401

www.wipfandstock.com

PAPERBACK ISBN: 978-1-7252-7286-6
HARDCOVER ISBN: 978-1-7252-7285-9
EBOOK ISBN: 978-1-7252-7287-3

Manufactured in the U.S.A.   10/15/20

*This book is dedicated with love and gratitude to
my wife, Vania, and my two sons, Mateus and David.
I so appreciate your patience, understanding, and support in the
writing process.
I always give thanks to God for your lives.*

I was hungry and you gave me food,
I was thirsty and you gave me drink,
I was a stranger and you welcomed me.

—MATTHEW 25:35

Contents

Foreword

The twentieth century was called the Age of the Refugee. As of this writing, that title can easily be applied to the twenty-first century as well. Turn on the news. Millions of people are fleeing for their lives, seeking asylum and refugee status. The United Nations High Commissioner for Refugees notes that nearly eight million people have been forcibly displaced from their homes, including at least twenty-six million who have been categorized as refugees. Around half of these refugees are under the age of eighteen.

People often ask me to share examples of churches doing ministry among refugees. They are hungry to learn from others. They desire to see a model and hear a story. If you are looking for an example of a church attempting to serve the refugees in her community, then this book is for you.

Jairo de Oliveira has produced this work to assist the body of Christ at a time when such assistance is most needed. This book not only calls us to open our eyes to the strangers next door from other nations but reminds us that refugee ministry is not just for large churches. Can a church of thirty-five members have an effective ministry to forty refugees? Absolutely! For here is the story of what God is doing through Arsenal Hill Presbyterian Church in Columbia, South Carolina, among refugees from Syria, Iraq, Congo, and Vietnam.

When I wrote *To the Edge*, I challenged readers to "Share Today's Stories Later Today," meaning that churches are not involved in a competition with one another. Churches do not create a research and development department like a corporation, keep silent, and then reveal successes with the world after years of ministry attempts. Wise kingdom citizens do not wait until everything is perfect before sharing with others. We do not go underground with an idea and practice before perfecting them and then launching them to the masses. Time is limited. Five billion people remain without Jesus. We must not wait but share our stories (including what needs to be improved) as soon as possible. This is exactly what the author attempts to do in this book! This is what we need to hear.

Drawing from years of personal experience and academic studies, de Oliveira helps us better understand some of the global realities, biblical teachings, and practical ministry steps related to refugees. Individuals and small groups will benefit from this book for each chapter concludes with helpful discussion questions, prayer points, and a call to action. The needs for ministry among refugees are great; the resources are few. I am thankful this work is now available to the masses.

Our Father is the Divine Maestro, orchestrating the movement of the nations for his glory (Acts 17:26–27). He works through the good migrations in life; he works through the plight of the refugee. He works through his people to bring the good news of the gospel across the street and across the world. A question for us is, "How should we respond since God has moved some of the world's most unreached people groups into our communities as refugees?" Here is a glimpse of how one church is answering this question. They have shared their story. May we learn from them. The need is great. The moment is now.

J. D. PAYNE, PhD
Pastor, missiologist, author of *Strangers Next Door: Immigration, Migration, and Mission*

Acknowledgments

Changing Stories is the result of a process that started years ago and involved many people. I am so pleased with its final form and pray that God will use it as a life-changing instrument. To all who have contributed, I am deeply indebted. First and foremost, I express my sincere gratitude to God, the Creator, LORD, Redeemer, and Refuge in whom my life is hidden with Christ. Many thanks to my professor Dr. David Cashin from Columbia International University for his esteemed guidance, advice, and encouragement during the writing process. I am also thankful for my friends Carla Foote, Jim Peterhoff, Rachel Turner, and Ruth Buchanan, for their invaluable assistance while reading, proofreading, and editing the manuscript. I am grateful for Columbia International University's faculty teaching, staff members, and students for the pleasant interaction and all the lessons I have learned from them while writing this book. I am indebted to my wife, best friend, and coworker, Vania, for standing beside me the whole time. I would not be able to conclude this work without her priceless support. Likewise, I am grateful for my sons Mateus and David, great partners in the ministry with refugees who always understand when there is a significant request for sacrificing family time to serve people who are in great need. I must also thank my local churches Segunda Igreja Batista na Taquara in Rio de Janeiro, Brazil, and Arsenal Hill Presbyterian Church in Columbia, South Carolina, for their example, fellowship, support, and encouragement at all times. I appreciate my refugee friends in Columbia from Syria, Iraq, Congo, and Vietnam, who have become like family. Their resilience before the tremendous suffering they have experienced in life is remarkable. I deeply admire and love them all. Finally, I would like to express my appreciation for my supporters, who have been investing in my life, ministry, and studies. I wish all cross-cultural workers would have such partners as I do.

Abbreviations

AHPC	Arsenal Hill Presbyterian Church
CIU	Columbia International University
ESL	English as a Second Language
ESV	English Standard Version
IDP	Internally Displaced People
ISIS	Islamic State of Iraq and al-Sham
ISV	International Standard Version
LSC	Lutheran Services Carolinas
NIV	New International Version
NKJV	New King James Version
PTSD	Post-Traumatic Stress Disorder
RHP	Refugee Highway Partnership
TEFL	Teaching English as a Foreign Language
TESOL	Teachers of English to Speakers of Other Languages
UNHCR	United Nations High Commissioner for Refugees
USC	University of South Carolina
WEA	World Evangelical Alliance

Introduction

We must pay attention to what is happening in the world. Our generation is facing an enormous and unprecedented migration crisis. The number of displaced people today is staggering. The current figures presented by the United Nations High Commissioner for Refugees (UNHCR) expose a disturbing picture our society cannot overlook. We live in a world where nearly eighty million people worldwide have been *forcibly displaced as a result of persecution, conflict, violence, or human rights violations.*[1]

The current migration crisis is one of the most critical issues and the biggest humanitarian challenge of our time. A crucial factor that aggravates the situation is the steady increase in the statistics of forcibly displaced people. According to UNHCR reports, the global population of forcibly displaced people has more than doubled in the last two decades,[2] directly impacting at least *1 percent of the world's population.*[3]

The migration crisis seems to be an endless catastrophe. When we look at Syria, we find an unbelievable picture. UNHCR estimates that the battles in the city of Idlib alone, in early 2020, left more than half a million displaced.[4] This incident represents one of the biggest waves of displacement since the beginning of the

1. UNHCR, "Global Trends: 2018," 2.
2. UNHCR, "Global Trends: 2016," 5.
3. UNHCR, "Figures at a Glance," figure 1.
4. The United Nations News, "Syria," para. 6.

clashes in 2011. This data reveals that the Syrian situation is getting further complicated due to an intricate conflict that looks like a never-ending war!

The world needs to realize that we are standing before an extremely complex situation. It is unpleasant to make chaotic predictions, but if we overlook the sources and outcomes of the ongoing migration crisis, it will probably require additional time, effort, and resources to come under control. As we look into the coming years and decades, the likelihood is that the refugee catastrophe currently striking our generation will continue to affect millions of lives. If this prediction is correct, the children of my children will also have to deal with a worldwide refugee crisis in their lifetimes.

While we analyze the current state of the migration crisis and the numbers that come with it, we must keep in mind that we are dealing with much more than just statistics. This crisis encompasses real people, some of whom are the most vulnerable in the world. Individuals who have been forced to leave their homes for reasons like "persecution, war, or violence."[5] Several men, women, and children are displaced in their own countries, while many others are scattered around the globe.

This challenging scenario speaks profoundly to me. The first time I experienced becoming an immigrant was in 1996 when I moved to South Africa to engage refugees from the civil war devastating Angola at that time. Since Brazilians and Angolans both speak Portuguese, Brazilians felt a moral obligation to help the thousands of refugees fleeing Angola and looking for shelter in South Africa.

My local church in Brazil, Segunda Igreja Batista na Taquara, recognized that God was specifically calling me to be at the front line of this challenge and sent me overseas, though I was only seventeen years old. I served among Angolan refugees in South Africa for over two years before returning to Brazil to continue my education.

Five years later, I resumed my work with displaced people in South Africa. After one year serving the refugees and learning English, I moved to other countries throughout the African

5. USA for UNHCR, "What is a Refugee?," para. 1.

continent. I ended up engaging refugees from the war in Darfur region, western Sudan, who were looking for refuge in different areas of Sudan and Kenya.

My most recent experience working with refugees is in the Middle East, where I am currently based. But, before establishing myself here, for approximately three years, I lived in the United States as an international student at Columbia International University. There I had the opportunity to work with resettled refugees from Syria, Iraq, Congo, and Vietnam. During this time, I served as a volunteer in the refugee ministry carried out by my local church there, Arsenal Hill Presbyterian Church, while conducting academic research for my Master's Degree.

This book flows from both my field experience and academic studies. The content represents an effort to examine the current migration crisis with a focus on the refugee crisis. As you move through the chapters, I pray you will join me as I will reflect on both crises from a biblical perspective, in an attempt to combine biblical theory and practice.

As you navigate in the pages of this book, you will find chapters permeated with stories of migrants from different backgrounds. Each story is unique and helps us hear voices representing hundreds of thousands of refugees who go unheard. They also challenge us to respond to the drama of people who are escaping from their homeland and moving across the globe as victims of armed conflicts, religious persecution, sexual abuse, and more.

Finally, I will analyze the refugee ministry that the Arsenal Hill Presbyterian Church is developing with refugees from Syria, Iraq, Congo, and Vietnam to help them rebuild their lives in every aspect. The analysis will use the *Best Practices for Christian Ministry Among Forcibly Displaced People* document proposed by the Refugee Highway Partnership as a framework.

As I discuss, reflect, and present the refugee ministry at Arsenal Hill Presbyterian Church, be aware that I do not intend it to be authoritative. I am not proposing a refugee ministry model to be seen as prescriptive but as descriptive. My purpose is not to offer you a set of formulas or a recipe to follow. Instead, I want to help you reflect on this learning experience and prayerfully consider how some of its characteristics can be translated into your own context of engagement with refugees, either within or beyond our borders.

Through this book, you will find answers to the following questions:

- How complex is the current migration crisis?
- What does the Bible say about displaced people?
- What are some of the available tools for a refugee ministry?
- How does a refugee ministry look like in a local church?
- What are some of the best practices for a refugee ministry?

May God be glorified as we join to reflect on the current migration crisis and act biblically on behalf of those who are displaced in their homeland or live as refugees in different parts of the world.

1

Each Person Has a Story

God loves each of us as if there were only one of us.

—Augustine of Hippo

On September 2, 2015, an appalling image shocked the world: that of a dead migrant child on a beach. Aged only two years, this Syrian boy, named Alan,[1] had drowned in the Mediterranean Sea and washed up on the Bodrum peninsula of southern Turkey. He died during a tragic attempt to leave the Middle East with his family. They'd been hoping to reach Europe by boat before traveling to Canada.

Alan's dead body, limp and lifeless, lapped by waves on the beach, directed fresh attention to the refugee crisis. Photographs of the boy wearing a red T-shirt, blue shorts, and dark shoes, lying face-down in the sand, made international headlines. This tragic incident sent a message to the whole world that the refugee crisis

---

1. Although the boy was reported on the media as Aylan or Aylan Shenu, all the names and ages of this Syrian family registered here are based on a family member's account, Tima Kurdi, Alan's aunt, as in her book, *Boy on the Beach*, xvii–xxvi.

is a serious matter. In fact, it is life and death. For many, this small Syrian boy embodied the drama of thousands of refugees escaping from persecution, war, or violence. Especially, those who continue to die after putting themselves at the mercy of precarious vessels to cross the sea.

Although the focus was placed on Alan, due to the graphic image, his death was not the only causality in this disastrous attempt to cross the Mediterranean. Sadly, his four-year-old brother, Ghalib, his mother, Rehanna, and nine other refugees died in that unfortunate event.[2]

On that Wednesday, Alan's family left the Turkish coast on an inflatable boat without appropriate life vests. Their flimsy rubber dinghy had a maximum occupancy of eight people, but it was carrying sixteen refugees. Only five minutes after they had set off for to the Greek island of Kos, a fierce storm blew over them. High waves broke against the overloaded boat. The frightened captain jumped into the sea in despair. Abdullah, Alan's father, tried to control the rubber dinghy with devastating consequences.

Some people may ask, "Why would refugees pay smugglers high sums of money to sneak them into Europe, navigate dangerous waters in unsecured boats, and expose the lives of themselves and family (including young children) to extreme risks?" Indeed, as Kurdi comments, "It may be impossible to comprehend unless you've lived the life of a refugee."[3]

Alan was a member of a Kurdish family. Because of his Kurdish origins, he became well-known as Alan Kurdi. The Kurds are the world's largest ethnic group without a country. They make up thirty million people living on the territory shared among Syria, Iraq, Iran, and Turkey. Kurds have been struggling to claim the right to have their own land for several decades. The troubling reality is that Alan and his family already come from a people group that has been scattered in different countries and is emblematic of the refugee crisis.

2. Brown, "3 Human Traffickers Each Jailed 125 Years," para. 4.
3. Kurdi, *Boy on the Beach*, xx.

Abdullah, Rehanna, Ghalib, and Alan were fleeing the Islamic State of Iraq and al-Sham. Their city, Kobani, in the Aleppo Governorate, was under siege by ISIS from September 2014 to January 2015. As a result, most neighborhoods were destroyed, and more than 160,000 people fled, fearing the ISIS fighters.

At first, the family did not intend to migrate. When forced to leave Kobani, they began moving between various cities in northern Syria in hopes of escaping the war. When they felt it was no longer safe to stay within the Syrian territory, they decided to cross the border. The family settled in Turkey, but they loved Syria and returned to Kobani at the beginning of 2015. Nevertheless, in June 2015, ISIS attacked the city again, and it became a battleground. They opted to take refuge in Turkey a second time. Life in Turkey was not easy for them, however. Their best option seemed to be to try to get to Europe and then to Canada, where they had family members living as immigrants.

This Kurdish family was longing for what most people desire in life. All they wanted was to cross the sea in their search to find peace, safety, a home, and a future. But their dream to live a better life sank with that boat on the Mediterranean.

After burying his wife and two children, Alan's father declared he wanted to go back to Syria. He did not wish to return because the war had stopped or because Syria had become a safe place to live. He changed his mind because the death of his family caused the loss of his dream. Abdullah's grief was so deep that he gave up his vision to find a better life in the West.

Unfortunately, Alan, his brother, his mother, and nine other refugees who drowned on that crossing attempt were not the last refugees to die while fighting to live. In 2019 alone, UNHCR estimated that 1,336 people perished in similar circumstances.[4] In almost all cases, their deaths rarely never make the international news, and we don't get a chance to hear their stories, but their blood is crying out. There remains much to be done to address the greatest humanitarian crisis of our modern history. Together, we can see these stories change.

4. UNHCR, "Global Report 2019," 126.

The migration crisis continues to force people out of their homeland in different parts of the world—people who share our humanity, our dreams, and aspirations. Refugees are humans like us who are enduring unimaginable suffering as a result of war, violence, persecution, food insecurity, climate change, infectious diseases (such as COVID-19), and many other factors. More than ever before, the international community must make every effort to guarantee their right to live and to live fully as people created in the image of God (Gen 1:27), unique and priceless.

GOD IS AT WORK

The current migration crisis involves people whose lives have turned upside-down as a result of the human rights violations they have experienced. Pain, suffering, trauma, disappointment, abuse, and exploitation follow them as they strive to carry on and rebuild their lives in unfamiliar contexts. As Sam George suggests, nobody can fully access all the terrible consequences related to the forcible displacement experience that refugees undergo: "Who will ever know the countless men, women, and children who drowned in the depths of the Mediterranean Sea or were buried in the deserts of Syria or Iraq? How could anyone assess the incalculable abuse and trauma refugees have suffered at the hands of violent gangs and border security forces as they sought shelter?"[5]

Although we are dealing with a tremendous challenge, unlike anything we have seen in the world, we must keep perspective and realize that nothing happens outside of God's intent and sovereignty. God knows everything, including each detail of our lives, "the very hairs of your head are all numbered" (Luke 12:7). Besides, nothing, good or bad, happens by accident, but by God's will, "Who can speak and have it happen if the LORD has not decreed it? Is it not from the mouth of the Most High that both calamities and good things come?" (Lam 3:37–38). Additionally, God reigns over everything, and the world is under his control: "The LORD reigns! He is clothed in majesty; the LORD is clothed, and he is girded

5. See George and Adeney, *Refugee Diaspora*, 298–99.

with strength. Indeed, the world is well established, and cannot be shaken" (Ps 93:1, ISV).

If we believe in the sovereignty of God, then we must conclude that these movements of people across the earth are not accidental. The migration crisis happens by God's permission and in harmony with the fulfillment of his kingdom purposes. As J. D. Payne affirms, "The Sovereign LORD orchestrates the movement of peoples across the globe in order to advance his kingdom for his glory."[6]

The Scripture teaches specifically that regarding all humankind, God is in control of their times and location so as to allow them to come into relationship with him, "From one man he made all the nations, that they should inhabit the whole earth; and he marked out their appointed times in history and the boundaries of their lands. God did this so that they would seek him and perhaps reach out for him and find him, though he is not far from any one of us" (Acts 17:26–27).

Indeed, God does not ignore the drama of people who have been displaced and are scattered around the world. Father, Son, and Holy Spirit are at work, and the movements of people are part of a divine plan to bring redemption to humankind, as the *Lausanne Diaspora Educators Consultation* acknowledged in their declaration published in 2009: "The sovereign work of the Father, Son, and Holy Spirit in the gathering and scattering of peoples across the earth is a central part of God's mission and redemptive purposes for the world."[7]

The current forceful human displacement has been scattering people who used to live in isolation from the gospel. Consequently, in their exile, they now have access to the Holy Scriptures. This changing scenario is affecting people who were previously considered unreached in the Middle East, for example, and are hearing the good news in countries like the Netherlands, Germany, England, the USA, Turkey, and Brazil.

Because God's ways are higher than our ways and his thoughts are higher than our thoughts (Isa 55:9), as we analyze the current

6. Payne, *Strangers Next Door*, 22.

7. The Lausanne Movement, "Seoul Declaration on Diaspora Missiology," para. 2.

migration crisis, we find God amidst the movements of people. He is doing a mighty work in the hearts of refugees, as George once again asserts, "God seems to be actively involved in drawing many refugees to himself."[8] Hence, the current refugee crisis is part of the bigger story that the LORD is writing over the centuries, and the results are impressive as, as Pam Arlund states: "In every country where we can gather information, many Muslims who have been engaged with the good news have responded favorably. From refugee populations, literally thousands (likely much higher) of new Muslim background believers (MBBs) have come into the kingdom."[9]

As a follower of the Messiah, I believe that God intervenes in the migration crisis because he has such a high commitment to life. One way he does so is by using those who believe, trust, and submit to him. Therefore, God has given his people a strategic position in the world and through them is fulfilling the Scripture that says: "repentance for the forgiveness of sins will be preached in his name to all the nations" (Luke 24:47). The *Lausanne Diaspora Educators Consultation* points out the church's role in the fulfillment of God's purpose to the world: "The church, which is the body of Christ, is the principal means through which God is at work in different ways around the globe."[10]

Thus, God is engaged in the task of letting everyone know about his marvelous works, and he uses the church to reach out to the nations. Since we received such a privilege, we must never forget that as believers in Christ, we are commanded to express his love to every individual in the world. "A new command I give you: Love one another. As I have loved you, so you must love one another. By this everyone will know that you are my disciples, if you love one another" (John 13:34–35).

8. See George and Adeney, *Refugee Diaspora*, 362.

9. See Arlund, "Opportunities and Threats in the Muslim World," loc. 917.

10. The Lausanne Movement, "Seoul Declaration on Diaspora Missiology," para. 3.

SHARING OUR FAITH

As Christians, we must respond to the refugee crisis because God rises when "the poor are plundered and the needy groan."[11] He is the one who declares, "I will protect them from those who malign them."[12] And we are called to fight evil by joining God in his acts of justice, "Defend the weak and the fatherless; uphold the cause of the poor and the oppressed. Rescue the weak and the needy; deliver them from the hand of the wicked" (Ps 82:3–4).

As we interact with refugees and become their friends, we don't control the outcome of their relational engagement with Jesus. However, as the Holy Spirit moves, sometimes we are instrumental in welcoming refugees into the family of faith, other times in fostering a desire in their hearts to examine our faith.

I remember when a Sudanese refugee once asked, "Tell me, who is Jesus? Who is Jesus to you? Is he God?" He broached the subject with a friend and me with these questions. He wanted to know more about the Messiah. As we began to answer, the Sudanese seemed confused. He was encountering such biblical knowledge for the first time. As our interaction progressed, a thought was running through my mind, "In two thousand years of Christian history, how in the world has the gospel not yet reached some people groups?"

Contact and relationship with people who have never heard the gospel still produces a sense of surprise and shame within me. How could I feel differently, considering the words of the apostle Paul to the Corinthians: "For some do not have the knowledge of God. I speak this to your shame" (1 Cor 15:34, NKJV).

The gospel access in some parts of the world is abundant, while in others is scarce. As disciples, we must follow the Master's example, as he distributed bread and fish to the crowd in the miracle of multiplication. The Scriptures teach that Jesus administered the food in such a way that they all ate (John 6:11). Similarly, we need to be open-handed as we share the gospel with the nations. Then, the remaining unreached people groups will be visited by the rising sun that came from heaven to "shine on those living in

11. Ps 12:5a.
12. Ps 12:5b.

darkness and in the shadow of death, to guide their feet into the path of peace" (Luke 1:79).

CAN WE SHARE OUR FAITH WITH REFUGEES?

Today, it is common to find people who are opposed to evangelism, even among Christians. In 2019, a report called *Reviving Evangelism* showed that 47 percent of practicing Christian millennials[13] say that Christians should not share their faith when relating to non-Christians.[14] Historically, however, Christians have understood that it is their responsibility to profess, live, and proclaim the good news of Jesus Christ to all people, in obedience to the Scriptures, "and you will be my witnesses in Jerusalem, and in all Judea and Samaria, and to the ends of the earth" (Acts 1:8).

Although, while it is biblical to share our beliefs with those we meet, as we interact with our refugee friends, we shall not perceive them only as people to be evangelized. We should not take advantage of their suffering as an opportunity to make new converts or use any privileged position to force them to embrace our confession of faith.

When we share the gospel with our refugee friends, we do it because we look to them as a whole—people who have a body, a soul, and a spirit. We long for them to experience a transformed life in each of these areas because we believe that Jesus can change their entire being for good.

Many verses from the Scriptures give us the solid confidence that it is biblical for Christians to share their faith with non-Christians. Nevertheless, do Christians violate non-Christians' human rights by sharing their beliefs with people like refugees? If we base our answer upon the Universal Declaration of Human Rights,[15] we can surely say that evangelism (or the proclamation of any other faith) is not against human rights. On the contrary, refugees have

13. The Pew Research Center defines millennials as people who were born from 1981 to 1996. See further Dimock, "Defining Generations."

14. See further "Millennials Oppose Evangelism."

15. United Nations, "Universal Declaration of Human Rights."

the human right of evaluating other faith expressions and even changing their religion if they freely so wish: "Everyone has the right to freedom of thought, conscience and religion; this right includes freedom to change his religion or belief, and freedom, either alone or in community with others and in public or private, to manifest his religion or belief in teaching, practice, worship and observance."[16]

Of course, in our interactions with refugees, we cannot be disrespectful, manipulative, or insensitive, but should always let them spontaneously choose if they want to hear the gospel and how they want to respond to it. As John Stott once said, "Christianity is not just about what we believe; it's also about how we behave."[17]

Likewise, the World Evangelical Alliance brings attention to the vital relationship between the centrality of the Christian witness and respect and love for people, as it was stated in a document called *Recommendations for Conduct* published in partnership with the World Council of Churches and the Pontifical Council for Interreligious Dialogue: "Mission belongs to the very being of the church. Proclaiming the word of God and witnessing to the world is essential for every Christian. At the same time, it is necessary to do so according to gospel principles, with full respect and love for all human beings."[18]

As we interact with refugees or any other group of people and preach the gospel to them, we must behave like people who know Jesus and are engaging others to love, welcome, and serve them.

EACH LIFE MATTERS

When we contemplate the extent of the migration crisis that is shaping our world and consider the circumstances affecting millions of displaced people, we could easily feel overwhelmed by the scope of the problem. Stunned by the statistics, we may lose our

16. United Nations, "Universal Declaration of Human Rights," article 18.

17. Stott, *Basic Christianity*, 15.

18. WCCPC World Evangelical Alliance, "Christian Witness in a Multi-Religious World," 3.

ability to care about the individual lives of those impacted when they are multiplied by such powerful factors. And we can lose heart regarding any action we might take as Christians following the call of Jesus in the face of a tremendous challenge.

Throughout this chapter, I share stories of displaced people. I have personally met all of them during the years I have worked with refugees. As I tell their stories, I intend to lift up their voices. I hope in listening to them, we will see our shared humanity and catch a glimpse of God's bigger story.

The accounts in the first section are from Syrian Muslim refugees who have been resettled to the United States and live in Columbia, South Carolina. They relate to the theme of war or violence as a consequence of the events unfolding in Syria for over a decade now. In the second section, you will meet Sudanese refugee women who have become Christians: their stories focus more on the theme of religious persecution.

Since persecution, war, or violence are key reasons for the massive numbers of people becoming refugees in the world today, the following stories illustrate their drama. For security purposes and confidentiality, their names and certain identifying details have been changed.

STORIES OF SYRIAN REFUGEES IN COLUMBIA

In 2016, my family moved from Nairobi, Kenya, to Columbia, South Carolina, in the United States. We moved there so that I could pursue graduate studies at Columbia International University. A few months after we arrived, my wife, Vania, and I got in touch with a group of refugees through our local church, Arsenal Hill Presbyterian Church.

Since we are a Brazilian family, we were also foreigners in the United States and did not have any family members in South Carolina outside of our nuclear family. Among other friends, the refugees became like a family to us. As we interacted with them and heard their stories, we came to know how much suffering they had experienced. By God's grace, they had escaped the ravages of war; though the war is still quite present in their lives. They always shared shocking stories of the conflict and exhibited ongoing stress. On one occasion, Zahara, who lost thirteen family members in a single weekend, reported, "I was on the phone with my relatives in Syria. Suddenly I heard the sound of an airplane and then of an explosion. As a result, the phone call was interrupted. Since then, I lost contact with my family members." An aircraft had bombed the area where some of her family members lived in Raqqa, which, at the time, was the Syrian capital of the Islamic State of Iraq and al-Sham (ISIS).

Not only do refugees carry the burden of concern about family in their home countries, but also the daily educational challenges their children face in their host countries. We all know that parents around the world share a common desire to nurture their children and give them the tools for life. Refugee families hope nothing less for their children, and they know education is an essential aspect of achieving this goal. However, after months following their arrival in the United States, most of the refugees were facing a hard time at school. The main problem was that they did not know English to understand everything taught in class. To further complicate the situation, the students could not receive help from their parents to do their homework because the whole family was at the beginning of their language acquisition process. Nevertheless, refugees remain tenacious and appreciative of the educational opportunities their crisis has afforded their children. Amina, another Syrian mother, told me once, "My priority is to help my children to succeed. My husband and I have lost our opportunity in life. I want my children to take advantage of the one they are having now. Otherwise, all our effort to be resettled here will be in vain."

In our interactions with refugee families, we have seen the sadness of parents who feel helpless at times concerning their desire to provide an appropriate educational experience for their children, even in hopeful situations. My wife's friend, Khadija, shared with us in a conversation, "At the end of the semester, my daughter had her graduation at the school, but I was not aware of the event. The school sent me a written communication, but I do not read English. My daughter told me that all the other mothers were at the graduation event, and she cried very much because I was the only one who was not there."

Anthropologists talk about various types of cultures. They usually make a distinction between cultures that are time-oriented and people-oriented.[19] In general, Syrians are not time-oriented but people-oriented. As a result, they value hospitality, something that should be characteristic of followers of Jesus as well. Consequently, it is impossible to visit a Syrian home and not spend time chatting and drinking one or two cups of coffee. Moreover, they never refuse a guest but instead, they give him priority in their schedules. When a guest is about to leave, they ask him to stay longer or to come back another day. Our friend Nadia seemed surprised by the differences between relationships and time management in America, "One difference between life in Syria and in America is in the area of relationships. People here are always busy, and they only give you a fraction of their time. When you want to visit a friend, you have to schedule an appointment. This is totally different in Syria." This particular cultural difference makes many refugees feel very lonely, especially at the beginning of their time in America. Refugees so appreciate when people show real interest in their lives and try to build friendship with them.

My interactions with refugees, who are among the most vulnerable people in the world, has enriched my life experience with maturity, wisdom, and perseverance. I am stunned by their kindness, generosity, and resilience in light of the great suffering they have experienced. Refugees are an example of daily overcoming. Day by day, they choose to fight for life, dream for a better future, and seek new beginnings.

Consequently, we must not assume that when we serve refugees, we are the ones giving, teaching, and comforting. They have much to share. Besides being generous and friendly, they have plenty of lessons to teach us. As we commit to serve them, we must do it with open hearts because we will probably receive much more than we can expect or give. In one way or another, our lives will likely be transformed. George Smith, an American friend who works with

19. Time-oriented cultures structure their priorities around the clock. People-oriented cultures give more focus to individuals and relationships.

Muslim refugees, told me once, "Some of them have become my best friends, and I can count on their help at any time. One Iraqi, in particular, if I can reach him at 2:00 AM, I know he will be there for me."[20]

While refugees report positive interactions with individual Americans, the threat of ISIS weighs on them. Some feel that people are suspicious of potential connections with terrorists. They often expressed fear of being associated with ISIS. Ahmed, a good friend of mine, tried to explain why it is not right to blame the Syrian people for the emergence of ISIS:

> The ISIS fighters are not from Syria. Abu Bakr al-Bagh-dadi, the founder of ISIS and its first caliph, was from Iraq. Many of his fighters are from different countries in Europe and North Africa. Most of ISIS fighters were for-eigners who went to Syria to fight for the terrorist group. The Syrian people are victims of these radicals. There-fore, it is not right to blame the Syrian people for the rise of ISIS. All that this group has brought to our people has been great suffering.

Though there are Christians among refugees from Syria, we've found that in Columbia, South Carolina, the majority of the Syr-ian refugees are Muslim. Some of them have shown concern about coming to the United States regarding practicing their faith. Mus-tafa, another Syrian man, stated, "I arrived in America with fear. While in a refugee camp in Jordan, I was warned by other Syrians to be careful because Americans would attack my faith. At some point, I was afraid to come to the United States, as I did not want to compromise my Muslim beliefs. But now I can see that I had no reason to fear. Americans are good people . . . and there is religious freedom here."

It must be extremely tough for refugees to be forced out of their homeland, lose some of their family members, and have to resume life on the other side of the world. How can they survive in a new context where almost everything seems different, where they have to make sense in a diverse culture and communicate in a new

---

20. Personal communication, November 12, 2017.

language? We can only come close to understanding this kind of life experience when we get to know them, build relationships, and hear their stories.

Across the globe, there are millions of migrants with their own stories—some similar to the Syrians, and some with twists based on their own backgrounds and circumstances. However, each refugee story is unique. Each human being has value and each life matters to God. Next, let us explore more stories of refugees I have met in my life journey.

STORIES OF SUDANESE REFUGEES IN NAIROBI

When I lived in Kenya, I had the opportunity to work with several Sudanese women who embraced the Christian faith in various ways during their exile. Next, let us explore their stories.

Aisha

Aisha was born to a prominent Sudanese Muslim family, though she did not grow up practicing Islam. She called herself a Muslim, yet she neglected to pray five times a day or fast during the Islamic month of Ramadan. At the age of fifteen, Aisha decided to approach Islam seriously. She concluded that since she was born into a Muslim family, she should be a Muslim and faithfully practice Islam. Aisha grew more involved with the local mosque and tried to observe everything the religion prescribes, but she found no peace and felt empty. One day, Aisha prayed and said to God, "Even though I belong to a Muslim family, I cannot be a Muslim, I was not born to be a Muslim. Help me to find my way."

After that, she started exploring how she could still please God with her life. Aisha realized she had Christians in her school and decided to ask them many questions. Then she went to a friend and shared her heart. As a result, Aisha's friend was able to explain the gospel in a way that Aisha did not previously know, and it seemed incredible to her. Ultimately, she embraced the Christian faith and surrendered her life to Jesus.

Aisha is now a Christian and has two major desires. First, she wants to grow in her new faith. Her goal is to be a mature Christian and explore all the blessings that God has for her. Second, she wants to see her family members experiencing the kingdom of God. She intends to share the gospel with her family and help them know Jesus, just as she does. Her favorite Bible verse is John 16:33, "I have told you these things, so that in me you may have peace. In this world you will have trouble. But take heart! I have overcome the world."

Rashida

Rashida was born in Sudan to a very traditional Muslim family. To this day, her father retains a high position in the army hierarchy and is a prominent man in the country. One day, a Christian friend gave Rashida a Bible as a gift. She was surprised to see a Bible for the first time. Fearing retaliation, she began reading the Holy Scriptures secretly. While Rashida came to the Gospel of John, God opened her spiritual eyes and allowed her to believe in everything the book was teaching about Jesus. Through faith, Rashida had a born-again experience and became very excited about serving Jesus. Her father heard about her decision to follow Christ and warned that if she didn't abandon the Christian faith, he would kill her. Rashida had no option but to run away to save her life. She left the country with her two sons and became a refugee in Kenya. When they arrived in Nairobi, all that they had were the clothes covering their bodies. Though she has faced much persecution, Rashida clearly demonstrates in every conversation that she is a vibrant Christian. As a matter of fact, she is still suffering persecution. Even though Kenya is a free country, her father is a man of power and has such influence that she lives under steady threats. In order to protect her life, she often moves from one city to another and starts life all over again. What seems astonishing, however, is that Rashida does not look at herself as someone in disgrace. She has found life in Jesus Christ and is a believer with a passion for her Savior. Wherever she goes, she proclaims her faith and becomes a source of encouragement to other refugees living in Kenya. She is an extraordinary woman who has been suffering joyfully for her faith. In one of our last interactions, she referred to 1 Peter 5:10, "And the God of all grace, who called you to his eternal glory in Christ, after you have suffered a little while, will himself restore you and make you strong, firm and steadfast."

Samira

Samira was born in Sudan but lived in Nairobi for two years during the time that I was based in Kenya. We lived in the same neighborhood, and I got in touch with her through a close friend who was also a Sudanese. She attended a Bible study I started and would often bring her family members to our gatherings. On my last night in Kenya, she came to my house to say goodbye and shared encouraging words, "In two days, after your family travels to Brazil, I will be returning to Sudan. I feel I have to go back home and share the gospel with my people. I want to share with them what I have learned from you." I was so excited to hear this. I could not believe Samira was about to become a witness to her own people.

As she concluded, I decided to ask her a question. I could imagine the suffering she was going to embrace for that decision, and I wanted to know if she was ready for that. Before asking the question, I reminded her that moving to Sudan was to return to a hard context. For decades, the government had been fighting Christians in the country. Then, I said, "I would like to ask you a question. Samira, do you not fear going back to Sudan, a place where you will be persecuted because of your faith?"

She answered, "The same God that is with me here in Kenya will be with me there in Sudan. God is here, and God is there. He will be with me, and I will be a true witness to my people." Then, she quoted Romans 8:38–39, "For I am convinced that neither death nor life, neither angels nor demons, neither the present nor the future, nor any powers, neither height nor depth, nor anything else in all creation, will be able to separate us from the love of God that is in Christ Jesus our LORD."

We cried and prayed together that evening. After Samira left, I thanked God for her willingness to embrace suffering and her desire to be a voice to her own people.

These are the stories of refugees—real people, loved by God, pushed from their homes, trying to establish new lives in a country with a culture and language different from their own. God is at work, both in them and through them, as they wander from place to place and sometimes manage to go back home.

As we contemplate the nations today, we see God touching the lives of strangers in surprising ways so that we are reminded of the words said to Habakkuk, "Look among the nations, and see; wonder and be astounded. For I am doing a work in your days that you would not believe if told" (Hab 1:5, ESV).

What does the Bible say about displaced people? How are we to think and engage with refugees in our midst? How does our story of faith intersect with the stories of these people? In the coming chapters, we will discuss these questions.

DISCUSSION QUESTIONS

1. Why is it important to pay attention to the migration crisis and consider that each person has a story?
2. How do you see God at work amid the current human displacement?
3. How are war and persecution influencing the current migration crisis?
4. Why do the Syrian refugees in Columbia see themselves as victims of ISIS?
5. So far, how have the individual stories of refugees impacted you?

PRAY FOR THE REFUGEES

Pray for each refugee around the world to find a place of refuge that offers a genuine opportunity for them to start a new life. Pray that God will give refugees the help necessary to overcome past experiences, find healing in every aspect, and develop a positive attitude toward life in their new context.

CALL TO ACTION

Write a paragraph about the most crucial lesson you have learned in this chapter and post it on your social media networks to bring your friends' attention to issues related to the current refugee crisis. If you want to connect with other readers of this book, use the hashtag #changingstories at the end of your post.

2

God's Story

The Biblical Basis for
Understanding Refugees

*We must be global Christians with a global vision
because our God is a global God.*

—JOHN STOTT

In one of our first interactions with refugees in Columbia, we met Safiya, an amiable Syrian mother. As she first looked at us, she got intrigued. Probably because of our seeming Middle Eastern physical appearance, Safiya correctly assumed that we were also away from home and asked: "Are you refugees too?" My wife, Vania, said no and explained what we were doing in Columbia, "At the moment, Columbia is our home, but we are from Brazil. We moved here so that my husband could study at Columbia International University. The visas we carry in our passports are a student and a dependent visa. So technically, we are not here as refugees."

For several days we discussed this question as a couple, "Can we consider ourselves refugees?" We knew it would be wrong and deceitful to introduce ourselves to people as if we were legally refugees in the United States. However, we always feel a special kinship with refugees, regardless of our country of residence. We say so because, as Christians, we believe we are "foreigners and strangers on earth" (Heb 11:13). Since we only live here momentarily, we are "longing for a better country—a heavenly one" (Heb 11:16), a place where we will dwell forever (Heb 13:14). Hence, my wife and I concluded that, in a sense, yes, we are refugees too. Regardless of our residency or nationality, all believers are like refugees who have been temporarily settled on this earth!

THE MIGRATION PHENOMENON

We live in a world that is in constant change. Historically, migration is one contributing factor that shapes civilization. It is an irremediable reality as Chandler H. Im and Tereso C. Casiño suggest: "The reality of the dispersion of individuals, families, and people groups on every corner of the globe is an irreversible phenomenon."[1]

The migration phenomenon is portraited in the Bible as well. Migration is a central aspect of the Scriptures, as we repeatedly see people movements from home to foreign contexts. Starting in the book of Genesis and moving to Revelation, we find men and women crossing territories and interacting with folks from other cultural contexts as part of their walk with the LORD. Jenny Hwang Yang brings attention to the biblical migration by saying, "Scripture is a story of people in exile and on the move, and many of the prominent characters in the Bible had a migration experience which was fundamental to their experience of God."[2]

The Holy Scriptures are not only filled with references about people in exile—living away from their homeland. They have much to say about caring for foreigners. Fortunately, the Bible has instructions for us today to deal with the migration crisis.

God is always with people on the move, and he wants us to partner with him in his work on the face of the earth. To help us

1. See Im and Casiño, "Introduction," 16.
2. Yang, *Global Diasporas and Mission*, 152.

effectively partner with God, we will now explore biblical teachings regarding people who live as pilgrims in a strange land.

THE FOREIGNER IN GOD'S EYES

God loves every human being without distinction. The Almighty is impartial toward people and has no prejudice for foreigners, "For the LORD your God is God of gods and LORD of lords, the great God, mighty and awesome, who shows no partiality" (Deut 10:17). God loves foreigners and openly declares his love for them, "He (God) loves the foreigners residing among you" (Deut 10:18). Furthermore, God commands his people to identify with him and love the foreigner as well, "And you are to love those who are foreigners" (Deut 10:19). As an expression of his love, the LORD makes provision for the foreigners, "giving them food and clothing" (Deut 10:18). God is on the side of the foreigner as the Almighty has his eyes on him: "The LORD watches over the foreigner" (Ps 146:9).

In the New Testament, we also find the truth that God loves without partiality. His love reaches out to people regardless of their religious, cultural, social, or linguistic backgrounds. God impressed this characteristic of impartiality about his nature to Peter through a vision, and Peter responded by saying, "I now realize how true it is that God does not show favoritism but accepts from every nation the one who fears him and does what is right" (Acts 10:34–35). The theologian Howard I. Marshall, explaining these verses on the Tyndale New Testament Commentary of the book of Acts, emphasizes that God loves all people and that he "does not have favorites."[3]

Stephan Bauman, Matthew Soerens, and Issam Smeir, leaders of World Relief, a Christian organization serving refugees globally, affirm in the book *Seeking Refuge* that refugees are equally precious and loved by God just like all the other human beings: "Each human being, regardless of ethnicity, gender, legal status, disability, or any other qualifier, is 'fearfully and wonderfully made' by the creator God (Ps 139:14), and as such has inherent

3. Marshall, *Acts*, 200.

dignity. We value and protect human life because we believe it is precious to God."[4]

God gave the breath of life to man and woman and wants to preserve the divine image retained in them and their descendants (Gen 1:26–28). The biblical description of humankind, as created in God's image, expresses that we all have equal value as people and reveals the highest view of humanity that we can find on the face of the earth. Moreover, the Bible is the oldest document in history that demands from a nation that their people had to love and treat the foreigner in the same way they treat their native-born, "The foreigner residing among you must be treated as your native-born. Love them as yourself" (Lev 19:34).

The pages of the Old Testament present a God sincerely concerned about people living away from home and experiencing vulnerability. As a result, God expresses his divine nature by instructing his people and shaping a society that will look after the foreigners—as Victoria Sielaff asserts, "God's character and love were designed to be lived out through his people by maintaining the highest level of community ethics, thus ensuring justice and dignity through hospitality for those who were non-Israelites living among them."[5]

God established in the land of Israel an unprecedented paradigm on how to relate to aliens. It was an entirely different pattern from the one the Israelites found in Egypt or Babylon. God was not only teaching Israel, but proposing to the whole world a just and compassionate model of care for foreigners.

In the Levitical Law, God makes a provision for those who do not own land and would be economically at risk, going so far as to set up the Jubilee year every fifty years (Lev 25). In that ancient system, God wanted his people to understand that they were actually to live as foreigners and strangers in the land that belonged to him, "The land must not be sold permanently, because the land is mine and you reside in my land as foreigners and strangers" (Lev 25:23).

4. Bauman et al., *Seeking Refuge*, 22.

5. See Sielaff, "Our Hospitality Mandate," 60.

The teachings the Israelites received on how to treat foreigners compelled them to have a broader perspective of God's plan for the nations. They would remember the foreigners in their acts of worship and desire that people from other cultures would come and worship God with them. One significant example is when Solomon is dedicating the temple in 1 Kings 8. He prays for foreigners who would hear about God and come and pray at the temple (1 Kgs 8:41–43).

In the Old Testament, the terms *alien, foreigner, stranger,* and *sojourner* are interchangeably used to describe people that we today call *immigrant*, for instance. The word originally used in the Hebrew Bible for all these terms is *ger*. According to the *Vines Expository Dictionary of Old Testament Words*, the word *ger* appears ninety-two times in the Hebrew Bible.[6] Interestingly, fifty-nine out of ninety-two times the word appears in the Torah—the collection of the first five books—which means that God emphasized the need for loving and caring for the foreigners when he was forming the nation of Israel and giving them the Law.

We must not assume that the word *ger* used in the Old Testament described a visitor or a tourist, to whom the Israelites had to extend hospitality. As Tim Keller argues, *ger* was "the outsider living in your midst."[7] In his book *Welcoming the Stranger*, Matthew Soerens expands this idea as he further explains the meaning of the word *ger* in the context of the Scriptures:

> Based on textual, historical and archaeological evidence, scholars believe that *ger* (in the context of the Hebrew Scriptures) refers to 'a person not native to the local area' and thus often without family or land; the same term is used to refer both to the Israelites when living (whether as welcomed guests or resented laborers) in Egypt as well as to non-Israelites living among the Israelites.[8]

Additionally, in an article entitled "Old Testament, Principles on Reaching the Refugee," Brenda Thompson, an assistant project

6. Vine, *Vines Expository Dictionary of Old Testament Words*, 371.

7. Keller, *Generous Justice*, 249.

8. Soerens and Yang, *Welcoming the Stranger*, 82.

director for the *State Refugee Project* in California, expands the application of the word *ger* to our days, "Our modern understanding of the word *refugee* is an equivalent of the Biblical definition of *ger*."[9] Hence the ones we call refugees today should receive the same treatment prescribed in the Scripture of the *alien, foreigner, stranger,* or *sojourner.*

Why were the Israelites instructed by God, in the Old Testament, to welcome the foreigners in their land and care for them? The main reason is that the Creator who loves foreigners would not allow his people to mistreat and oppress them, "When a foreigner resides among you in your land, do not mistreat them" (Lev 19:33). Furthermore, the Israelites had been foreigners in Egypt. They knew how tough it could be for people to live in a foreign context. Thus, God wanted them to show compassion and generosity for the strangers living among them, "And you are to love those who are foreigners, for you yourselves were foreigners in Egypt" (Deut 10:19). Joel Green highlights how important it was for the Israelites to treat people based on the lessons they learned in life: "The Israelites must never forget that they had been despised foreigners in another land. At one time, they had been workers in Egypt's oppressive system, but they had been redeemed by God's gracious, powerful hand. That is, as descendants of immigrants, they should be generous to the sojourners among them."[10]

In the Old Testament, we also find laws given to the Israelites that would refer to and include strangers. Apparently, their faith and religiosity were not disconnected from the reality that foreigners were residing among them, as we see in Leviticus 16:29–30, "This is to be a lasting ordinance for you: On the tenth day of the seventh month you must deny yourselves and not do any work—whether native-born or a foreigner residing among you—because on this day atonement will be made for you, to cleanse you. Then, before the LORD, you will be cleaned from all your sins."

9. Thompson, "Old Testament, Principles on Reaching the Refugee," 364.

10. Green, *Dictionary of Scripture and Ethics*, 163.

A PEOPLE IN EXILE

The Old Testament has much to teach about people living as foreigners or refugees. The Israelites were not only displaced when they turn out to be slaves in Egypt. At other times in biblical history, God's chosen people experienced the unfortunate reality of being forced out of their land to become pilgrims in another nation. On one occasion, they were taken captive to Babylon and remained there for seventy years, "He carried into exile to Babylon the remnant, who escaped from the sword, and they became servants to him and his successors until the kingdom of Persia came to power" (2 Chr 36:20). While they were scattered, they experienced continuous oppression and homesickness, "By the rivers of Babylon we sat and wept when we remembered Zion" (Ps 137:1).

Thus, on more than one occasion, we find Israel as a nation in exile. The diaspora of Jews exiled from Israel has not been limited to events in the Old and New Testaments. It continued to happen after biblical times. Following the destruction of Jerusalem in AD 70, the Jewish community was forced to spread, and several leading centers of Judaism were established outside their homeland.[11]

According to the *Oxford Dictionary*, diaspora is the "dispersion or spread of any people from their original homeland."[12] The concept of diaspora can be extremely broad and applied to immigrants, refugees, and other groups living away from their original contexts.

In addition to the experiences of dispersion faced by people groups, we find Israelites who individually had to leave their land and move to another country. For instance, migration was part of God's plan for Abraham when the Almighty gave his servant the promise, "I will make you into a great nation" (Gen 12:2). God told Abraham to leave his country and move to a new land, as we find in Genesis 12:1, "The LORD had said to Abram, 'Go from your country, your people and your father's household to the land I will show you.'"

---

11. "Diaspora Judaism," para. 3.
12. Stevenson, *Oxford Dictionary of English*, 485.

Another important person who became a foreigner was Joseph, when his brothers sold him to Midianite merchants. The Midianites took Joseph to Egypt to sell him as a slave, "So when the Midianite merchants came by, his brothers pulled Joseph up out of the cistern and sold him for twenty shekels of silver to the Ishmaelites, who took him to Egypt" (Gen 37:28). God not only allowed, but also used this incident of unjust human trafficking to preserve his people. Many years later, there was a famine in the world, and Joseph's whole family became refugees in Egypt as they sought food in the land of the pharaohs.

The Old Testament also talks about Moses, who had the experience of becoming an alien. Moses's experience as a foreigner in Egypt was so remarkable that it affected the name he chose for his firstborn son, "Zipporah gave birth to a son, and Moses named him Gershom, saying, 'I have become a foreigner in a foreign land'" (Exod 2:22).

The name Gershom contains the Hebrew word *ger* (foreigner). *The Word Biblical Commentary* explains that the name Gershom is connected with "stranger" and "there."[13] Therefore, in naming his son Gershom, Moses was pointing to the great significance of his diaspora experience and highlighting its magnitude for future generations.

In the Scripture, we also find Ruth, the Moabitess, who married an Israelite from Bethlehem. After Ruth's husband and his brother died, she followed her mother-in-law, Naomi, who had experienced the loss of her husband too, as she moved from Moab back to Bethlehem. As a consequence, Ruth became a foreigner among the Israelites. By God's grace, she married Boaz and experienced favor and redemption in a time of sorrow and famine (Ruth 4:9–13). Interestingly, Ruth represents one of the four foreign women who is included in the lineage of Jesus of Nazareth (Matt 1:5).

There are still plenty of examples in the Old Testament. I will mention just one more of a young man called Daniel, who was taken with his friends to Babylon: "Among those who were chosen were some from Judah: Daniel, Hananiah, Mishael and Azariah" (Dan 1:6). Fulfilling God's plan, Daniel and his friends made a significant

---

13. Durham, *Word Biblical Commentary*, 23.

impact in the country of Babylon through their faithful obedience to the God of Israel.

PRACTICAL BIBLICAL INSTRUCTIONS FOR CARING FOR THE FOREIGNERS

The LORD cares for the foreigners, providing for their material needs. He does so by giving them food and clothing, as we already saw. As a consequence of his loving character, God presents instructions in the Torah by which the people of Israel were to care for foreigners. Hence, caring for foreigners or refugees had more implications than just sharing the land with them.

By caring for foreigners, the Israelites would express their priesthood as a nation, since they were divinely called to reveal God's attributes to the strangers living among them and to the entire world. So, regarding the foreigners they were asked to:

- **Treat them well** (Exod 22:21): "Do not mistreat or oppress a foreigner, for you were foreigners in Egypt."

- **Show them benevolence** (Lev 19:10): "Do not go over your vineyard a second time or pick up the grapes that have fallen. Leave them for the poor and the foreigner. I am the LORD your God."

- **Share spiritual blessings with them—such as forgiveness** (Num 15:26, ESV): "And all the congregation of the people of Israel shall be forgiven, and the stranger who sojourns among them."

- **Love them** (Deut 10:19): "And you are to love those who are foreigners."

- **Offer them a portion of the tithe** (Deut 14:28–29): "At the end of every three years, bring all the tithes of that year's produce and store it in your towns, so that the Levites (who have no allotment or inheritance of their own) and the foreigners, the fatherless and the widows who live in your towns may come and eat and be satisfied, and so that the LORD your God may bless you in all the work of your hands."

- **Respect their rights** (Deut 24:17): "Do not deprive the foreigner or the fatherless of justice or take the cloak of the widow as a pledge."
- **Teach them God's Word** (Deut 31:12): "Assemble the people—men, women and children, and the foreigners residing in your towns—so they can listen and learn to fear the Lord your God and follow carefully all the words of this law."

Moreover, the biblical account teaches that some of God's blessings were conditional. Blessings would be given to the Israelites based on the way they treated the foreigners and other vulnerable people represented in their society: "if you do not oppress the foreigner, the fatherless or the widow and do not shed innocent blood in this place, and if you do not follow other gods to your own harm, then I will let you live in this place, in the land I gave your ancestors for ever and ever" (Jer 7:6–7).

INSTRUCTIONS FOR THE FOREIGNERS LIVING AMONG THE JEWS

As counterparts, in order to live a blessed life and enjoy the benefits the people of Israel had to offer, foreigners were to obey the same laws and rules that governed the country, "The community is to have the same rules for you and for the foreigner residing among you; this is a lasting ordinance for the generations to come. You and the foreigner shall be the same before the Lord: The same laws and regulations will apply both to you and to the foreigner residing among you" (Num 15:15–16). By giving foreigners the same laws, God was certainly protecting them from discrimination.

They were not forced to convert or to practice Judaism; however, if they did so, they would be required to follow identical rules as the people of Israel regarding religious practices, "And if a stranger shall sojourn among you and would keep the Passover to the Lord, according to the statute of the Passover and according to its rule, so shall he do. You shall have one statute, both for the sojourner and for the native" (Num 9:14, ESV).

Non-observance of the precepts given by God could cause severe consequences for foreigners as much as for Jews. One such result was to be cut off from the people, "And you shall say to them, any one of the house of Israel, or of the strangers who sojourn among them, who offers a burnt offering or sacrifice and does not bring it to the entrance of the tent of meeting to offer it to the LORD, that man shall be cut off from his people" (Lev 17:8–9, ESV).

REFUGEES IN THE NEW TESTAMENT

Besides reinforcement of the teachings of the Old Testament, we find in the New Testament that Jesus, Joseph, and Mary went into exile. The Gospel of Matthew tells us that right after Jesus was born, Herod wanted to kill him. To escape this threat, Joseph left their homeland with Mary and Jesus and fled to a place of refuge. "So he got up, took the child and his mother during the night and left for Egypt" (Matt 2:14). This circumstance placed Jesus and his parents in a situation of displacement that today would be considered as the formal status of refugees. As Edward Smither underlines, "Because of their forced displacement due to political tyranny and genocide, Joseph's family fits the modern definition of a refugee."[14]

The picture of Jesus of Nazareth seeking refuge in Egypt sends a powerful message to the millions of refugees scattered around the world today, as Stephan Bauman, the president of World Relief, states: "The millions of refugees in our world today have an advocate in Jesus, who was 'made like them, fully human in every way' (Heb 2:17), able 'to empathize with our weaknesses' (Heb 4:15)—even with the particular experience of having to flee one's home in the middle of the night in search for refuge."[15]

The theologian Fleur Houston adds, "Jesus can empathize with refugees in their sufferings, enables endurance, and brings hope."[16] Also, the fact that Jesus left exile and, at the appropriate

---

14. Smither, *Christian Martyrdom*, 4.

15. Bauman et al., *Seeking Refuge*, 32.

16. Houston, *You Shall Love the Stranger as Yourself*, 136.

time, returned to his homeland (Matt 2:19–21) can be a significant factor and an instrument of hope for the refugees of our time.

We find that the principles revealed in the Old Testament are reaffirmed in similar New Testament teachings about caring for foreigners. Like the Jews, Christians are instructed to offer hospitality to the stranger, "Do not forget to show hospitality to strangers, for by so doing some people have shown hospitality to angels without knowing it" (Heb 13:2).

We find in the Gospels clear instructions for the disciples to love and care for needy people, which today certainly applies to the refugee. When a certain lawyer stood up and asked Jesus, "Who is my neighbor?" (Luke 10:29). In reply, Jesus told him the story of the "Good Samaritan" who reacted with love and compassion for the man he found half-dead on the side of the road from Jerusalem to Jericho. Then, Jesus told the lawyer, "Go and do likewise" (Luke 10:37). In other words, Jesus was telling the man to show love and compassion toward those who crossed his way in vulnerability and desperate need.

Moreover, when referring to the judgment of the nations, Jesus teaches that those who will inherit the kingdom of God are the disciples who served him: "For I was hungry and you gave me something to eat, I was thirsty and you gave me something to drink, I was a stranger and you invited me in, I needed clothes and you clothed me, I was sick and you looked after me, I was in prison and you came to visit me" (Matt 25:35–36). Jesus further explains to the disciples that we serve him by taking care of those whom he calls brothers and sisters: "'LORD, when did we see you hungry and feed you, or thirsty and give you something to drink? When did we see you a stranger and invite you in, or needing clothes and clothe you? When did we see you sick or in prison and go to visit you?' The King will reply, 'Truly I tell you, whatever you did for one of the least of these brothers and sisters of mine, you did for me'" (Matt 25:37–40).

The strangers represent one of the groups of people in need that Jesus mentioned to the disciples in the passage. Thus, whenever we invite them in, we are inviting Jesus; and whenever we serve one of Jesus' brothers and sisters, we are serving him.

CHRISTIANS AS REFUGEES IN THIS WORLD

It is particularly relevant to consider that even though Jesus went back to Israel after his exile in Egypt, he was never attached to a particular place. "Jesus went through all the towns and villages, teaching in their synagogues, proclaiming the good news of the kingdom and healing every disease and sickness" (Matt 9:35). Therefore, Jesus was not based in his hometown of Nazareth; nor did he establish a geographic place as his permanent home. Jesus began his earthly ministry at the Jordan River with his baptism and ended it in Jerusalem from where he ascended to heaven. Indeed, there were times when he had no shelter and no place to lay his head (Matt 8:20). Jesus was in the world, but he did not belong to the world, "For I have come down from heaven" (John 6:38).

Jesus's example illustrates an important concept that applies to the Christian community as well. In the Old Testament, the Israelites received land from God to inhabit, but in the New Testament, God's people do not have a physical land as a sign of their covenant with the Almighty. As a consequence, God's people are like foreigners or pilgrims on the face of the earth, as Peter highlighted in his writings: "Dear friends, I urge you, as foreigners and exiles" (1 Pet 2:11).

The New Testament also states that Christians' "citizenship is in heaven" (Phil 3:20). Consequently, the Scriptures assert that people who follow Jesus are like sojourners because they are not of the world, even if they have received an earthly passport and citizenship: "They are not of the world, even as I am not of it" (John 17:16). Hampton J. Keathley III highlights that Christians are aliens on earth, instead of everlasting residents: "We must not settle down as 'earth dwellers' who live as though this world were our permanent home or all there is to life. You know the attitude I am talking about—'we need to get all the gusto we can because we only go around once.' Instead, believers in Christ should live as temporary residents whose citizenship and real home is in heaven."[17]

As we recognize the millions of refugees living in exile in different parts of the globe, we need to keep in mind our identity

17. Keathley, *ABCs for Christian Growth*, 360.

and position in this world as followers of Jesus. We are people who found refuge in Christ and became citizens of God's kingdom by grace alone. Therefore, we must empathize with individuals who are scattered and welcome them in the place where God has given us our transitory residence.

PEOPLE ON THE MOVE

The reality of people moving around is not new, and it often comes to light throughout biblical history. One significant biblical account is registered in the book of Acts. On the day of Pentecost, the Holy Spirit was sent to the disciples in the context of people on the move: "Now there were staying in Jerusalem God-fearing Jews from every nation under heaven. Parthians, Medes and Elamites; residents of Mesopotamia, Judea and Cappadocia, Pontus and Asia, Phrygia and Pamphylia, Egypt and the parts of Libya near Cyrene; visitors from Rome (both Jews and converts to Judaism); Cretans and Arabs" (Acts 2:5, 9–11).

Jews and converts to Judaism from all nations were attracted to Jerusalem every year to celebrate the feast of Pentecost, as Brian Hébert argues: "At the time of Pentecost, there were dozens of nations represented in the diaspora that were 'pulled' to Jerusalem for the religious festival."[18]

God knew very well what he was doing when he decided to send the Holy Spirit during the Jewish feast. Every nation was represented in Jerusalem. Therefore, it was the perfect occasion for the disciples to receive the Holy Spirit as the heavenly power was sent to make them witnesses of Jesus Christ to the world: "But you will receive power when the Holy Spirit comes on you; and you will be my witnesses in Jerusalem, and in all Judea and Samaria, and to the ends of the earth" (Acts 1:8).

The dispersed people who came to Jerusalem witnessed a singular manifestation of God's power and signs. Following that, three thousand among them decided to entrust their lives to Jesus as they responded to Peter's preaching and were baptized (Acts 2:41).

18. See Hébert, "Respondendo ao Fenômeno da Imigração," 108.

The new believers who left Jerusalem and went back to their nations witnessed the wonders of God to their people, making a tremendous impact in different regions, as Edward Smither asserts, "Since vibrant church communities sprang up in these same regions in the first few centuries, it's very likely that these believing Jewish pilgrims returned home proclaiming their newfound faith in Christ."[19]

Furthermore, church history was developed in the context of migration. The dispersion of early Christians through persecution allowed the gospel to be preached broadly, as we see in the book of Acts: "those who were scattered went everywhere preaching the word" (Acts 8:4, NKJV). Historians have affirmed the centrality of migration, through persecution and other means, to the story of the spread of Christianity, pointing out that since the beginning, the church has been subject to dispersion, as Smither once again highlights:

> From the first century to the present day, the mission of God has continually been carried out in the diaspora context. At points in Christian history, immigrants, refugees, and displaced peoples have migrated to a place where they heard the gospel and became part of the church. At other times, Christians themselves have moved or been displaced and have had a witness among the nations as a result.[20]

The dispersion of early Christians and the current displacement of refugees[21] reflect certain similarities. We find God using the movement of people in both scenarios to promote the gospel's progress across the world.

---

19. See Smither, "Um Olhar Histórico sobre Diásporas," 32.

20. See Smither, "Um Olhar Histórico sobre Diásporas," 31.

21. The International Organization for Migration defines displacement as "the movement of persons who have been forced or obliged to flee or to leave their homes or places of habitual residence, in particular as a result of or in order to avoid the effects of armed conflict, situations of generalized violence, violations of human rights or natural or human-made disasters." See International Organization for Migration, "Key Migration Terms," definition for "Displacement."

WELCOMING THE STRANGER

Considering aspects like scriptural evidence and church history, Christians should have a distinct perspective on migration. Furthermore, they should be the community of faith most prepared to welcome the stranger in our day. However, I often find Christians resisting the idea of caring for the foreigner. I confess that I am confused by this scenario. Perhaps one of the roots of this problem is a lack of solid biblical theology about migration among our people. Unfortunately, many Christians around the world and in the United States do not know their Bible and history well enough regarding this critical issue. Maybe another root of the problem is disobedience to the Scriptures, which would then be much worse than a lack of knowledge. In general, human nature prefers pleasure rather than discomfort. Therefore, in our days, where the philosophical concept of hedonism is so strong, we find a greater tendency to follow the biblical teachings only in areas that make us feel comfortable. As a result, we compromise allegiance to scriptural obedience in areas that make us uncomfortable, like loving those who look different or are strangers. Also, we tend to read our cultural paradigms into Scripture, when instead, we should be allowing Scripture to challenge our cultural paradigms in many issues, such as loving the foreigner. We definitely need the Holy Spirit to teach, change, and transform our hearts.

Nevertheless, as we fulfill our mission in the present century, as a church, we must consider migrants. We cannot refuse to welcome those who God is bringing from afar and those who he is leading mightily into the kingdom as a part of our family.

As people who seek to obey God, we must serve him among the refugees not only because they are in need, but also because the Almighty commanded that we do so. Thus, refugee ministry is more than a matter of helping the stranger. Ultimately, it is a matter of obedience to God.

DISCUSSION QUESTIONS

1. Why can Christians be considered refugees in this world?
2. Why does God demand that his people welcome the foreigner?
3. What are some of the practical ways that the Israelites were called to embrace and serve the foreigners?
4. What did you learn regarding foreigners in the New Testament?
5. How is God specifically speaking to you about refugee ministry?

PRAY FOR THE REFUGEES

Pray that God will shelter the refugees trying to cross their borders and give them the opportunity to move to a safe place. Pray that God will put committed Christians in their way who will love, help, to meet their essential needs, and boldly proclaim the gospel to them.

CALL TO ACTION

Share the content of this chapter with your pastor and church leaders. Ask them if the church has a plan to engage the refugees in your context and discuss the possibility of your church getting involved with refugees.

3

The Current Story

The Twenty-First-Century Refugee Crisis

*Millions of people are on the move today—more than
ever before in our planet's history.*

—Patrick Johnstone

Maya was born in a Yazidi village in Sinjar district, northern
Iraq. In 2014, when she was fifteen, her people were attacked
by a group of ISIS fighters. ISIS wanted to wipe out the Yazidis.
The terrorists considered Maya's people as *infidels* and *devil wor-
shippers*.[1] The ISIS fighters who carried out the attack took control
of the village and slaughtered most men and older women. Maya
and many other girls were taken captive. The terrorists kept young

---

1. Yazidis are a people group originally from Iraq, Syria, and Turkey. The
Yazda and the EAMENA Project points out that Yazidis "inherited their identity,
faith, culture and tradition from their ancestors. The only way to become Yazidi
is to be born from two Yazidi parents. A core tenet of the monotheistic Yazidi
faith is the belief that Xuada (God) created the world, including Lalish, in seven
days and entrusted it to seven holy angels, including Tawûsê Melek, who Yazidis
believe to be the head of the angels. Yazidism is divided into three sects: Merid,
the general population, and the religious Pir and Shix sects." See Yazda and the
EAMENA Project, "Yazidi Cultural Destruction Report 2019," 28.

Yazidi women alive for a single reason: they planned to make them sex slaves.

When ISIS fighters finished the executions, they took the young Yazidi women, including Maya, to the city of Mosul. Their destination was a slave market where the girls would be sold to other ISIS terrorists.

On the same day that Maya was offered at the market, a twenty-seven-year-old militant bought her. He paid the equivalent of sixty dollars, a third of his weekly salary as an ISIS soldier. Maya was sold for that sum because she was still a virgin. Otherwise, she could have been sold for half that price.

When Maya arrived at her new home, she experienced great cruelty. The young girl was beaten and raped several times. The brutality continued over the following days, weeks, and months. About seven months later, Maya had lost much weight. Her body was weak, as well as her soul and spirit. Then, the ISIS soldier decided to sell Maya to another young militant for a much lower price than he had paid for her.

The young girl was taken by her new owner to live in a house with two other Yazidi slaves. Once again, Maya became a victim of mistreatment and sexual exploitation, but now at least she had the companionship of other Yazidi girls.

Four months later, she was sold a third time to a much older man to be his only sex slave. Although Maya represented no threat whatsoever, once again, she was handled with physical violence and sexual abuse. Maya would often ask herself as she wept in the darkness, "Why is this happening to me? What have I done to deserve all this suffering? How can I get out of this?"

One night, Maya found an opportunity to escape. Her new "owner" got ill and was not able to keep the girl under his watch. Maya managed to sneak the housekeys from the man and use them to gain her freedom. She boldly locked her captor in the house and ran for her life to the main street. Stopping a taxi driver, she breathlessly asked for help. Filled with compassion, the taxi driver agreed to help her. Maya told him that she had a brother living in Turkey, and the man decided to take her to the Turkish border, about two hours away.

Once Maya entered Turkey, she was able to reunite with her brother. She shared with him all the suffering she had experienced and heard in more detail about the massacre that had happened to her people in other Yazidi Iraqi villages. Six months after Maya's arrival in Turkey, she managed to get to Europe. Since then, Maya has connected with the Yazidi diaspora established in Germany.

We have seen that movements of people through their respective diasporas is an issue repeatedly occurring throughout world history, from ancient times to the present. As Brantley Scott affirms, "Since the beginning of time, humanity has been leaving one home and looking for another. Adam and Eve, Joseph and his brothers, Moses, Jesus and his early earthly family, and the early apostles, such as Paul, were always on the move, both voluntarily and involuntarily."[2]

Although diaspora is not a new and unknown phenomenon to humankind, it has never influenced the lives of so many people as it does today. The numbers expressed by the current migration crisis corroborate that the reality of people experiencing diaspora has never been so prevalent as in our days. By *diaspora*, we want to consider not only the refugees, but all the other groups of migrants living away from their original contexts.

Here, we look at the complexity of the current migrant crisis, consider the factors that are contributing to the problem, and discuss the implications of the crisis in the lives of people and societies around the world.

A CHALLENGING SCENARIO

We live in a historical moment. The dispersion of people in the world has reached unprecedented proportions. The numbers registered by UNHCR reveal that nearly eighty million people are forcibly displaced worldwide.[3] The Christian organization World Relief

2. See Scott, "Migration & Diaspora," 66.
3. UNHCR, "Global Report 2019," 2.

describes the current forcibly human displacement as "the greatest, most complex humanitarian crisis of our generation."[4]

To understand the current migration crisis, we need to recognize that mainly three groups comprise the large category called *forcibly displaced people (FDPs)*. The groups are: *internally displaced people (IDPs), refugees,* and *asylum seekers.*

Forcibly Displaced People

The largest population among the forcibly displaced people is the *internally displaced people*. Over forty-five million people live in this condition.[5] The United Nations High Commissioner for Refugees classifies IDPs as "people or groups of people who have been forced to leave their homes or places of habitual residence, in particular as a result of or in order to avoid the effects of armed conflict, situations of generalized violence, violations of human rights, or natural or man-made disasters, and who have not crossed an international border."[6]

In a context marked by war, the IDPs leave their homes but still remain within their own borders and under the authority of their government. This happens even if the government is the very source of their displacement. For various reasons which include but are not limited to old age, poor health, or lack of money; they have not managed to cross their country's border. Consequently, they are relocated somewhere within their own territory, whether or not the war still affects their lives in some way. Given these conditions, though they are refugees, they may never have a chance to be considered so officially or be resettled overseas.

Refugees

The second-largest group of forcibly displaced people is conventionally called *refugees*. Today, at least twenty-six million people

4. World Relief, "Respond," para. 8.
5. UNHCR, "Figures at a Glance," figure 1.
6. UNHCR, "Global Trends: 2016," 56.

are living under this designation.[7] The 1951 Geneva Convention defined a refugee as a person who, "owing to a well-founded fear of persecution for reasons of race, religion, nationality, membership of a particular social group or political opinions, is outside the country of his nationality and is unable or, owing to such fear, is unwilling to avail himself of the protection of that country."[8]

A disturbing distinction that demands attention is the fact that refugees are among the most vulnerable people in our era. Dr. Rajeev Bais from the University of South Carolina has developed various medical initiatives to assist refugees in the United States. One of them is called Carolina Survivors Clinic.[9] Based on his experience providing medical services to refugees, he says, "There's nobody who has gone through more trauma and witnessed the worst that humanity has to offer than a refugee." Dr. Bais makes another comment on the suffering that some refugees have experienced as victims of torture and human rights abuse: "There is one girl who's[sic] father was murdered, whose mom was raped. Her sisters were raped and she was raped, and this was not just once, but multiple times . . . All of her sisters got pregnant from rapes. She got pregnant and had a kid, and then she found out she was HIV-positive. And this is a 17-year-old girl. Can you imagine?"[10] Sadly, such a plight is not uncommon for those labeled *refugees*.

Asylum Seekers

The third segment of forcibly displaced people is the *asylum seekers*. They are the smallest group represented in the migration crisis, according to how UNHCR categorizes forcibly displaced people. UNHCR estimates that over four million people live in this condition worldwide.[11] Amnesty International defines an asylum seeker as "an

7. UNHCR, "Figures at a Glance," para. 1.

8. International Organization for Migration, "Key Migration Terms," definition for "Refugee."

9. University of South Carolina, "Healthy New Start," para. 8.

10. University of South Carolina, "Healthy New Start," paras. 6–7.

11. UNHCR, "Figures at a Glance," figure 1.

individual who is seeking international protection. In countries with individualized procedures, an asylum seeker is someone whose claim has not yet been finally decided on by the country in which he or she has submitted it. Not every asylum seeker will ultimately be recognized as a refugee, but every refugee is initially an asylum seeker."[12]

In general, the term *asylum seeker* is used by different organizations to refer to people who are seeking, but have not yet received, international protection. In some cases, this would include people whose claims for refugee status have not yet been determined.

Refugees sometimes fall under the status of an asylum seeker. For instance, refugees who live in a refugee camp in a host nation that cannot integrate them may apply for asylum. In this case, they will look for a third country willing to host them.

The refugee crisis is actually a crisis within the greater migration crisis. The UNHCR figures acknowledge that there are more people (almost double) displaced inside their own countries (internally displaced people) than around the world (refugees).

The current displacement of peoples has produced significant pressure in two distinct contexts. First, there is some pressure in the countries causing the massive outflow of refugees. Second, nations hosting refugees also experience some kind of pressure. The Syrian situation and some of its consequences vividly illustrate the reality of this dynamic.

THE SYRIAN DRAMA

Although problems related to persecution, war, or violence are happening in many nations across the globe and forcing people to leave their country, Syria is an epicenter of the current migration crisis. At the time of this writing, this Middle Eastern country is responsible for sending out the most significant number of refugees to the world.[13]

The displacement of the Syrian people is a result of the ongoing civil war that has torn apart the country. Many Syrian cities

12. Amnesty International, "What's the Difference," para. 1.
13. UNHCR, "Global Report 2019," 141.

have been destroyed, and more than half of the country's population have been displaced. The numbers resulting from the Syrian crisis are astounding, Christopher Phillips asserts, "The Syrian civil war is the greatest human disaster of the twenty-first century. Since conflict broke out in 2011, over 470,000 have been estimated killed and 1.9 million wounded. Over 4.8 million have fled the country and 6.6 million more are internally displaced."[14]

One of the major consequences of the human tragedy happening in Syria is its impact on children. It is disheartening that around half of the nearly twenty-six million refugees are under the age of eighteen.[15] Another effect that this crisis has on children is the number of unaccompanied and separated children crossing borders worldwide. In recent years, the number of children trying to find refuge on their own in a country they don't know has been increasing.[16] Will they be able to explore the world and find refuge without their parents, any relative, or a legal guardian?

The sad reality is that most of these refugee children, living without adult protection, are subject to circumstances that involve a high risk of being abused.

THE WAR IN SYRIA

The twenty-first century's biggest war really began on March 15, 2011, but Syria was officially proclaimed to be in a state of civil war by the United Nations on June 12, 2012.

Following the uprisings, known as the Arab Spring, in countries such as Tunisia, Libya, and Egypt; Syrians took the streets and began to protest against their president Bashar al-Assad. They were unhappy with their political leader, who at that time had been in power for eleven years. Bashar al-Assad became the Syrian president on July 10, 2000, after receiving the command of the nation from his father, Hafez al-Assad, who had been ruling the country for almost thirty years.

14. Phillips, *Battle for Syria*, 1.
15. UNHCR, "Figures at a Glance," para. 1.
16. UNHCR, "Global Trends: 2018," 49.

People opposing Assad claimed to be tired of Syrian ruling regime, which was considered to be authoritarian in their understanding. Hence, they wanted the establishment of a new government that would give more voice to the people. Unfortunately, Bashar al-Assad forces violently reacted to the people's protests, arresting a group of teens and children in the suburbs of Daraa and killing dozens of people. The violence spread and divided the country. As Jonah Pierce recounts, "Violent clashes between government security forces and protestors intensified, as demonstrators increasingly armed themselves."[17]

One of the Syrian refugees I met in South Carolina shared with me his impressions of how the war started: "We went to bed one night, and when we woke up the next morning, the war was before our eyes."

At the time, the opposition formed a coalition called the Syrian National Council to fight the government forces. The tension escalated to levels that destabilized the country. In the meantime, in June 2014, Abu Bakr al-Baghdadi declared himself a caliph[18] at the Great Mosque of al-Nuri in Mosul, Iraq.[19] He formed a group called the Islamic State of Iraq and al-Sham (ISIS). Taking advantage of the chaotic situation in the region (Syria and Iraq), they established Raqqa as the capital city of their "caliphate"[20] in Syria. As a result of these combined events, Syria has been devastated, giving rise to a disaster that the United Nations calls the biggest humanitarian emergency of our era.[21]

As the numbers point out, the displaced Syrian population is enormous. Syrian refugees and asylum seekers are scattered everywhere. After all the suffering they have experienced, many of them are struggling to survive. They need help to find viable solutions to overcome their current situation and carry on.

---

17. Pierce, *Anissa of Syria*, 3.
18. A ruler over all Muslims in the world.
19. Atwan, *Islamic State*, 111.
20. The Muslim state headed by a caliph.
21. Edwards, "Needs Soar," para. 7.

SOLUTIONS

The migration crisis deals with the reality of people who are losing everything: their home, their family members, and their country. As refugees, many of them have no safe place, no food, and no money. Also, they cannot return to their country because once again, they would face life threats. As people who have freedom, shelter, and food on the table, we must look up from our comfort and recognize that refugees exist, look after them, and find solutions to address the humanitarian crisis they are facing.

What are some of the short and long-term solutions we need to consider to address the refugee crisis? In general, UNHCR identifies two kinds of solutions that can apply to refugees and asylum seekers. They are divided into short-term and long-term solutions. Next, let us take a look at some of these and examine their effectiveness.

SHORT-TERM SOLUTIONS

Short-term solutions are important responses to crises in general. They tend to provide different types of humanitarian aid, which can save lives and temporarily alleviate the suffering of those who are in agony.

Although short-term solutions may need to be renewed on a regular basis, as long as they are necessary, they are essential to mitigate the consequences of a crisis, "When violence erupts or war breaks out, life can change in a matter of minutes—shattering families and communities and driving millions to flee."[22]

Sometimes, short-term initiatives are carried out by specialized relief workers, like medical professionals, who are always ready to step up immediately in a crisis context. Other times, short-term efforts are made by volunteers filled with compassion; people willing to offer their time, money, and skills to serve others who are facing dangerous situations.

Some examples of short-term solutions are:

22. UNHCR, "Emergency Relief Efforts," para. 1.

Humanitarian Aid

Humanitarian aid is a temporary solution, which is intended to save, protect, and maintain lives. Many refugees depend on humanitarian relief actions, which benefit them by providing shelter, food, and medication, among other resources. Organizations specializing in humanitarian relief operations usually have a trained work team, but accept volunteers to join hands and serve in specific areas as well.

Short-Term Residency Permits

Escaping war can be just as traumatic as facing war itself. Therefore, refugees need assistance in the process of getting to a safe place. Therefore, a valuable temporary solution that aids in this task is short-term residency permits. They are given by governments and allow refugees to be documented as they stay in a country for a specific time or move across borders trying to get to a particular country.

Refugee Camps

Refugee camps are designed to provide "temporary shelters built to accommodate refugees, migrants, and asylum seekers."[23] They can be as populated as many metropolises. Kutupalong Refugee Camp, in Bangladesh, is the largest in the world. It hosts nearly a million refugees, mostly Rohingya people fleeing Myanmar.[24]

Although temporary in principle, many refugees live in refugee camps for several years. Usually, the refugees living in camps have no idea how long they will be stuck there before moving on with their lives.

---

23. "Key Terms About the Refugee Crisis," para. 5.
24. UNHCR, "Saving Lives," para. 6.

LONG-TERM SOLUTIONS

Many Syrians have left their country and no longer have family members, close friends, or a safe home in Syria. What could be some of the long-term solutions for people facing this kind of situation? In a quick definition, a long-term solution is a tangible proposal to provide protection and opportunity for a new life for people who have been displaced. UNHCR defines a durable solution for refugees as "One that ends the cycle of displacement by resolving their plight so that they can lead normal lives. Seeking and providing durable solutions to the problems of refugees constitutes an essential element of international protection, and the search for durable solutions has been a central part of UNHCR's mandate since its inception."[25]

UNHCR understands that there are three long-term or durable solutions that can change the future of refugees and asylum seekers, as we find next.

Voluntary Repatriation

The best scenario regarding durable solutions is when refugees are able and willing to return voluntarily to their homeland. UNHCR calls this *voluntary repatriation* and defines it as "the return in safety and dignity to the refugees' country of origin, based on their free and informed decision."[26]

Many refugees desire to return to their home countries where they may regain control over their lives in a familiar context. Between November 2018 and January 2019, UNHCR interviewed Syrian refugees in its fifth Refugee Perceptions and Intentions Survey in Egypt, Iraq, Jordan, and Lebanon. UNHCR people asked Syrian refugees if they were willing to return home. The majority of them, precisely 75 percent, expressed their desire to return to Syria eventually.[27]

25. UNHCR, "UNHCR Resettlement Handbook," 28.
26. UNHCR, "UNHCR Resettlement Handbook," 31.
27. UNHCR, "Global Trends: 2018," 217.

Refugees, by definition, are not people who leave their country because they wanted to migrate, but because they are forced out of their territory. It naturally follows that their homeland is the place to which they feel they belong.

The biggest challenge for most refugees wishing to return home is that of insecurity. While conflicts remain ongoing in countries affected by war, voluntary repatriation is not a viable option. In such contexts, for voluntary repatriation to become a reality, a combined effort to cease war and rebuild the country is necessary.

Local Integration

If refugees cannot go back home because the situation in their original country brings risk to their lives, another viable solution is local integration. Local integration is intended to integrate refugees in their host contexts, namely the countries where they are living temporarily. For example, it is likely the country that hosts their refugee camp.

UNHCR defines local integration as a permanent settlement of the refugees. "Local integration, in which refugees legally, economically, and socially integrate in the host country, availing themselves of the national protection of the host government."[28]

Local integration is an effective long-term solution, and it is a process that leads "eventually to permanent residency and, in some situations, to naturalization."[29]

One of the biggest challenges to refugee integration is that some countries that host refugee camps do not have the capabilities of hosting enormous numbers of refugees. Integration of all refugees in such nations requires a vast infrastructure. Also, it produces a significant change in the local context. "Local integration is a complex and gradual process, comprising three distinct but interrelated dimensions, legal, economic, and socio-cultural."[30]

28. UNHCR, "UNHCR Resettlement Handbook," 28.
29. UNHCR, "UNHCR Resettlement Handbook," 34.
30. UNHCR, "UNHCR Resettlement Handbook," 413.

Some countries that host refugees temporarily, especially in the Middle East and Europe, are already overwhelmed with the refugee demand. Part of their population is feeling the country has done enough and cannot take more refugees. Others are still willing to integrate displaced people.

Resettlement

The third durable solution is resettlement. Resettlement is an opportunity for refugees and asylum seekers to be transferred to a new country "which has agreed to admit them as refugees with permanent residence status."[31]

Resettlement involves removing people from a context to a new setting where they will be able to secure normal living conditions, settle down, and resume their lives.

Resettlement is not a new solution. This paradigm was initially established to protect refugees during the Second World War. "UNHCR made extensive use of resettlement as a means of resolving the situation of finding solutions for European refugees after the Second World War."[32]

Resettlement is a crucial solution for refugees. According to the UNHCR professionals who are much experienced in dealing with displaced people, "Resettlement is recognized today as a vital instrument of international protection, integral to comprehensive protection and durable solutions strategies."[33]

Although it has historically been a viable long-term solution, not many countries are willing to take in refugees for resettlement. As a result, a minimal number of refugees are actually ever resettled. UNHCR asserts that less than 1 percent of refugees are resettled each year.[34]

When a refugee gets a chance to resettle in the United States, for example, he is assigned to one of the six national resettlement

31. UNHCR, "UNHCR Resettlement Handbook," 3.
32. UNHCR, "UNHCR Resettlement Handbook," 47.
33. UNHCR, "UNHCR Resettlement Handbook," 47.
34. UNHCR, "Resettlement," para. 2.

agencies, such as Lutheran Services Carolinas. The resettlement agency is responsible for preparing the refugee's transition, organizing his international trip, meeting him at the airport on his arrival to the country, and assisting him in his integration process.

THE PROCESS

First, it is important to note that only refugees and asylum seekers can be resettled, not economic migrants.[35] Thus, people who are eligible for resettlement are those who have been persecuted because of "race, religion, nationality, membership of a particular social group or political opinion."[36] Consequently, they are forced to leave their homes and cross a border looking for safety. Sometimes, before looking for a refugee camp, they live displaced for years within their own country, looking for ways to protect their lives.

Regarding resettlement in the United States, it is not an easy or a quick process. It can take over twenty months, which is a long wait for people who have experienced the worst life can offer and who continue to deal with different kinds of suffering.

After leaving a war zone, for example, and crossing a border, the person looks for an office of the United Nations High Commissioner for Refugees to register and receive the official refugee status. Then, an important step in the process starts: the person must prove he or she is a refugee and not just someone trying to take advantage of the process to migrate overseas. At this point, the UNHCR focuses on collecting enough information to determine if the person claiming to be a refugee can prove that deserves to be under international protection. Before receiving authorization to settle in a refugee camp or an urban environment, the person will

35. According to Amnesty International, an economic migrant as "someone who leaves his or her country of origin purely for financial and/or economic reasons. Economic migrants choose to move in order to find a better life and they do not flee because of persecution. Therefore, they do not fall within the criteria for refugee status and are not entitled to receive international protection." See Amnesty International, "What's the Difference."

36. International Organization for Migration, "Key Migration Terms," definition of "Refugee."

undergo a screening process and be required to provide biographic information, biometric data, and identifying documents. Also, UN-HCR personal will conduct interviews with the person and ensure that she meets all the requirements to receive the refugee status.[37]

Once refugees arrive in America, they must undergo security checks one last time by a Customs and Border Protection (CBP) officer to verify that they have the proper documentation. After going through security, they meet members of the local resettlement agency and other volunteers who will welcome the refugees into the country and help them begin their journey in the United States.

RESETTLEMENT AGENCIES

Collaborating in this process, there are resettlement agencies in the United States which serve to facilitate the introductory experience of the refugees in the country.

Once the refugees arrive, the resettlement agencies have a large task, especially in the first six months. They must count on the help of their partner organizations and volunteers to get the job done. Together, they organize the family's arrival, set up a house, and welcome the family at the airport. Next, they assist the refugees in obtaining documentation, opening a bank account, and signing contracts. They offer cultural training, transportation for interviews or pre-employment screenings, and so on.

Organizations such as churches, universities, and schools partner with resettlement agencies so that together they can provide all the services the refugees need.

This is where we need to help and join this long-term solution. We need to take part in the resettlement process and seek to assist our refugee friends in areas that will help them to be self-sustaining instead of being dependents relying on our assistance.

---

37. The United States Committee for Refugees and Immigrants, "Security Screening of Refugees Admitted to the U.S."

RESETTLEMENT AND THE ISSUE OF TERRORISM

Besides other challenges, some of the refugees navigating the globe are originally from countries where there is significant terrorist activity. For instance, they come from nations like Iraq, Afghanistan, and Syria, which are among the top five countries where terrorism is taking place in the world, according to *The Global Terrorism Index*.[38]

Terrorism is a serious and widespread problem in our days. Muslim fundamentalists represent the leading groups involved in this kind of violence, while not the only ones if we take a broader look at what terrorism means. However, since the tragic events of September 11, 2001, terrorism has become the highest threat to national security for most governments around the world—even more so in Western countries. In an article published in 2017 by *The Washington Times*, Americans considered terrorism the number one problem facing the United States: "Americans now name terrorism, more than any other issue, as the most important problem facing the country."[39]

A significant concern in the United States and many other countries is whether their authorities are allowing terrorists to move to their land as they open the borders to resettle refugees.

The good news is that embracing refugees does not necessarily represent a security threat as many people may think. David Houston, a State Department spokesman, highlights that there are stringent security measures taken before allowing refugees to enter the country: "Refugees are the most thoroughly screened category of traveler to the United States . . . and Syrian refugees are subject to even more scrutiny."[40]

To enter the United States as a refugee requires a long process. For a refugee to be admitted in the country is much more complex than most people may think. Lutheran Services Carolinas area manager, Lindsey LeDuc, clarifies how the process takes place: "Becoming a refugee in the United States demands two application stages, and it can take up to twenty-four months to be completed.

38. World Atlas, "Global Terrorism Index," table 1.
39. Sherfinski, "Terrorism Most Important Problem Facing U.S.," para. 1.
40. McKinney, "Eleven Syrian Refugees Now Call Columbia Home," para. 11.

Both stages take place while the refugee is still overseas, waiting to be resettled. It is a long process, longer than all the other immigration processes."[41]

Also, refugees are required to undergo screening procedures to prove they do not represent any threat regarding health and security, for example. As for security, whenever it is necessary, intelligence agencies get involved in the process to make sure they are not linked to terrorist groups or terrorist activity. Refugees are cleared and allowed to travel to the United States only after they have been approved in all the procedures.[42]

The reality is that a country can welcome the stranger and, at the same time, implement necessary security measures in the resettlement process. Likewise, it is viable for a Christian to respond biblically to the alien next door and, at the same time, encourage and preserve the nation's security.

We have seen how God's story of interaction with his people has intersected with refugee stories throughout history. In our present day, the movement of people is not a surprise to God, and he is providing the church with tremendous opportunities to show his love to the refugees in their midst. To focus all our attention on whether or not refugees should be allowed to enter our country is not helpful. As God's people, our main concern should be how we treat the refugees who are already our next-door neighbors.

The push and pull factors of the migration crisis have displaced millions of people in our days, refugees like the Yazidi Maya. As a result, they are now coming to us because the place they used to call home no longer exists. Their country has been destroyed, their society is in complete disorder, and their world is shaken. Therefore, let us be gracious to the afflicted and extend our hands to the needy. Let us care for individuals like us who are moving in our direction, hoping to find acceptance, shelter, and a new beginning.

41. Meeting at Arsenal Hill Presbyterian Church on January 15, 2017.

42. See further the United States Committee for Refugees and Immigrants, "Security Screening of Refugees Admitted to the U.S."

DISCUSSION QUESTIONS

1. Why can diaspora not be counted as a new phenomenon?
2. What are the short-term solutions for the refugee crisis mentioned in this chapter?
3. Which of the long-term solutions do you think is the most effective? Why?
4. Do you agree that embracing refugees does not necessarily mean a security threat concerning terrorism? Why or why not?
5. In which capacities could you serve and care for the refugees around you?

PRAY FOR THE REFUGEES

Pray for the countries that are at the center of the refugee crisis. Pray for the end of the civil war and armed conflicts that are causing death, wounds, and the displacement of millions of people. Pray that God will raise good leadership in these nations, people willing to be peacemakers, and make decisions for the benefit of the people.

CALL TO ACTION

Find out how many refugees are in your area. If you are in the United States, use the website *Refugee Processing Center* to verify the numbers of admissions and arrivals of refugees in your state for a specified period: http://ireports.wrapsnet.org. Next, send a text message to all your contacts with the number of refugees in your area, followed by the phrase: "God loves refugees!"

4

Their Story

Understanding Refugees and
Responding to Their Needs

The world does not understand theology or dogma,
but it understands love and sympathy.

—Dwight L. Moody

Farida flew for the first time in an airplane when she was nine years old. She was not traveling to visit family abroad, spend a vacation overseas, or explore one of her favorite places. Farida's first airplane ride was to the United States where she and her family would be resettled as refugees.

Farida was born in Homs, Syria. When she was only five years old, war erupted in her hometown, the third-largest city in Syria at the time. In just a few months, various clashes and airstrikes produced widespread panic, destruction, and death. Her neighborhood changed drastically, becoming a war zone.

As a result of the chaos, Farida's family had no other choice but to leave Homs. How could they continue living their daily lives within the context of a violent war?

Farida's father was a taxi driver who knew very well how to get out of the city. But where would he take his wife and seven children? The best idea seemed to be to run with his loved ones to the capital city of Damascus.

After four consecutive days of armed conflicts that shook their city, came a ceasefire. The family understood it was the right time to escape. When darkness fell, they fled. Before they were able to take the highway to Damascus, they drove through the outskirts of Homs, headlights off. They wanted to stay unnoticed in case of snipers.

As they made their way to Damascus by traveling forty-two miles, which passed through a city called Qara, they sensed their lives were out of danger. After months feeling that death was sitting at their doorstep, this was a fresh and welcome relief. As they considered what life would be like ahead, all they assumed that living amid war was an experience they had left behind.

Unfortunately, their worst nightmare was still on the horizon. Ten months after they settled, over a hundred miles away from home, the war also came to Damascus. To their despair, history did not just repeat itself: their situation actually became even harder than what they had experienced in Homs. In a bomb explosion, Farida lost her older brother, Mustafa, who was seventeen years old. He was killed on his way home after playing soccer with friends. At that point in her life, Farida had lost more than twenty people from her extended family. They died as a consequence of the conflicts that were popping up in different parts of Syria.

Once again, the war was showing its terrifying face. Violence surrounded them, placing their lives at continuing risk. Now, instead of remaining as IDPs, they felt compelled to flee their home country completely.

On their way to exile, Farida and her family joined other Syrians in a caravan. They went south, heading toward the Jordanian border on a ninety-two-mile journey. The journey started in pickup trucks and finished on foot. They were looking for shelter at the world's largest camp for Syrian refugees, Zaatari Refugee Camp, which is *home to over seventy-six thousand people.*[1]

After they crossed the border, Farida's parents asked themselves if they would ever go back to Syria or see the loved ones they had just left behind. They did not have an answer and left the future with God *"Insha Allah,"* which in Arabic means, if God wills it so.

Settling down at the refugee camp was a bittersweet experience. They were happy to be out of the war zone but concerned about the living conditions there. Farida's father was shocked to hear that he would probably not be able to find a formal job. He was told that *at Zaatari less than 20 percent of the refugees have active work permits.*[2] As a man who started working when he was ten years old, he longed to make his own money and support his family.

Surprisingly, despite the extreme trauma caused by the war, including the grief they felt after losing their firstborn, Mustafa, Farida's parents were still able to dream for a better life. They had the strength to carry on and the initiative to explore permanent solutions to change their living conditions.

Nevertheless, as a result of the frequent explosion of bombs in Damascus, Farida's mother developed Post-Traumatic Stress Disorder (PTSD), and her father lost about 70 percent of his hearing ability. The medical challenges the couple faced decreased their ability to care for their children, making them particularly vulnerable.

For the sake of everyone's health and well-being, it was clear the family needed to be resettled. But their very status as refugees posed an obstacle: *As refugees, they could not initiate the process or even apply for resettlement.*[3] They had to be identified as eligible through UNHCR for resettlement and then be *selected by a government for lawful admission.*

When Farida's family was about to complete her ninth month living at the camp, her parents were called to a regular meeting with

1. UNHCR, "Jordan: Zaatari Refugee Camp," para. 2.

2. UNHCR, "Jordan: Zaatari Refugee Camp," para. 6.

3. Resettlement under the auspices of UNHCR involves the selection and transfer of refugees from a state in which they have sought protection to a third state that has agreed to admit them—as refugees—with permanent residence status. See UNHCR, "Frequently Asked Questions about Resettlement," 7–8.

the UNHCR staff members. Following their standard operating procedures, they wanted to review the needs of each member of the family. As the staff members heard about the parent's health condition and how it was affecting their children, they grew concerned. First, the staff had to confirm the accuracy of the information they had received by consulting other members of their field office. After doing that and taking all the required steps, the UNHCR staff members concluded that this family needed international protection and should be assigned for resettlement.

Two months later, Farida's family was filled with joy when they received communication telling them that *UNHCR had officially recognized and submitted their case for resettlement.* The first step toward resettlement was accomplished. Now, the next step was to be selected by a government willing to allow them legal immigration. The fact that *refugees cannot pick their country of resettlement* did not bother them. As long as they moved to a context where they could rebuild their lives, they would be pleased.

At times, it was hard for them to believe they had been appointed to receive the benefit of resettlement. It seemed just like a dream! They knew that *less than 1 percent of the world's refugees ever get resettled worldwide,*[4] making them lucky to have been selected to be part of this small and sad statistic.

As all families do, they also had disappointments. One day, a neighbor told them that *refugees usually spend eighteen to twenty-four months sitting at a camp waiting for the completion of their resettlement process.*[5] When they first learned this, they certainly could not imagine themselves waiting for so long. In the end, the process took the time their neighbor had predicted. Farida and her family waited twenty-two interminable months *being interviewed and completing the required medical and security screening process.*

Patience is truly a virtue, and this family demonstrated the ability to wait without losing hope. To their amazement, during the summer of 2015, they got good news. The American government had selected them to be resettled in the United States. Just a few

4. UNHCR, "Resettlement," para. 2.
5. Refugees Northwest, "By the Numbers," para. 2.

days later, the whole family left their tent at one of the twelve districts in Zaatari. From there, they went to Queen Alia International Airport, in Amman, to depart for America.

Once they crossed the Atlantic, they discovered that life in the West was not as easy as they thought. The family struggled tremendously at the beginning of their resettlement experience in the United States. Farida's father changed jobs three times within the first six months. Her mother discovered she had arthritis and wrestled with joint pain until she found proper treatment. The children suffered to make friends at school. However, they were all able to eventually find their way. With help from one of the American Resettlement Agency and a neighborhood church that was a community partner, they managed to make the necessary adjustments.

During her second year in the States, Farida started to thrive in school and became very dedicated to her academic studies. At the time of this writing, she has just finished middle school with excellent grades. When she thinks of a future career, her dream is to become a medical doctor to provide health care to people and save lives.

Farida has not flown on an airplane since she first flew with her family to the United States. She says that her next international trip will be after graduation from medical school. Once she becomes a doctor, she would like to visit the Zaatari refugee camp in Jordan to serve as a short-term volunteer. Since the civil war still does not allow her to assist her people inside Syria freely, she wants to do something for Syrian refugees who have not yet been resettled.

Wouldn't it be interesting if Farida's next international trip takes her back to the very place where her family's dream to become resettled began?

What you just read is based on a true story. It was used to illustrate how the process of resettlement takes place. It is fantastic that Farida and her family got the chance to be resettled and that a church was involved in the process once they got to America!

Christians have expressed different reactions regarding the resettlement of refugees among them, and it is not different when it comes to Muslim refugees, as Pam Arlund points out: "In countries where Muslims have resettled, Christians have had varied reactions. Many have reacted out of suspicion and fear and reacted only to the threat they feel Muslim immigrants present. Others have reacted to new Muslim neighbors as an opportunity to engage Muslims with the good news and love of Jesus."[6] Fortunately, there are churches and believers individually that are choosing to overcome negative reactions and express God's love for refugees.[7]

In this chapter, I will give you an outline at different aspects of the life of a specific group of refugees, Syrians living in Columbia, South Carolina, and show other examples of churches involved with refugee ministry around the world.

ENGAGING REFUGEES IN COLUMBIA

My relationship with Syrian refugees in Columbia started in August 2016, when I moved to the city with my family in order to study at Columbia International University. During the same time, Arsenal Hill Presbyterian Church (AHPC) received a new pastor, Reverend Robert Turner. Along with his family, he had just moved back to the United States after twelve years serving with World Witness in Turkey. Reverend Turner had the vision of a multiethnic ministry for his church. He intended to help his congregation to reach out to all kinds of people with the gospel, regardless of their background. The pastor wanted to promote God's glory to his city by proclaiming salvation, reconciliation, and unity that can be found only in Jesus and expressed in the body of Christ (Gal 3:28).[8] Based on his previous experience in Turkey with Iranian and Iraqi refugees, he was determined to embrace the refugees in Columbia.

---

6. See Arlund, "Opportunities and Threats in the Muslim World," loc. 917.

7. See Morgan, "1,180 Churches Help World Relief."

8. Arsenal Hill Presbyterian Church, "Our Roots," para. 3.

I got in touch with the AHPC about four weeks after my arrival in the United States. I quickly became a member of the congregation, and joined the work there as well.

The church started their refugee ministry on October 30, 2016, embracing twenty-nine Syrians from four different families. After some time, Iraqi, Congolese, and Vietnamese refugees were added to the group, raising the number of refugees to over forty.[9]

The main service the church provides to the refugees is free English as a Second Language (ESL) classes, covering cycles of six to nine weeks. The classes happen on Sunday afternoons and serve men, women, boys (middle school and high school), girls (middle school and high school), and children (elementary and nursery).

All participants running the program are volunteers, mainly from three groups: church members, Columbia International University students and staff, and University of South Carolina students and staff.

UNDERSTANDING THE SYRIAN REFUGEES

To provide an overview of the specific audience to whom the church is ministering, I conducted an ethnography (a systematic study of people and cultures) of Syrian refugees, which were the majority group. The ethnography was a prerequisite of one of my classes, called Understanding Cultures and Worldviews at Columbia International University.[10] I felt it would be valuable to integrate this class requirement to the refugee ministry and decided to conduct the interviews that took place from January 2017 to May 2017. Some information reported on the ethnography I collected during my interactions with the Syrian refugees, which started in October 2016.[11] Prior to the formal interviews, I built relationships with all participants through the ESL program run by the AHPC and visits to their homes.

9. Personal notes from the evaluation meeting at Arsenal Hill Presbyterian Church on January 15, 2017.

10. A class taught by professor Dr. David Cashin.

11. Only a portion of the ethnography is incorporated in this chapter.

THE SYRIAN REFUGEES AT THE ESL PROGRAM

The Syrians were resettled in Columbia by Lutheran Services Carolinas, a private resettlement agency affiliated with Lutheran Immigration and Refugee Service. They are the partner agency working with the AHPC. Lutheran Services Carolinas works to connect refugees with communities, organizations, and people who are willing to help them transition to a new life in the United States. In their own words, "Lutheran Services Carolinas welcomes refugees and immigrants and helps them transition into a new life and a new culture."[12]

All Syrians assisted by the church spent years in one of the refugee camps in Jordan, either Azraq or Zaatari. After staying at these camps, they were able to apply for resettlement in the United States. Azraq was opened in April 2014, while Zaatari started providing shelter to refugees in July 2012. Both refugee camps were established specifically to address the needs of Syrian refugees fleeing violence from the Syrian civil war that erupted in 2011.

The Syrians who were interviewed were born in the Syrian Arab Republic, a country that is located in the Middle East and shares borders with Iraq, Israel, Jordan, Lebanon, and Turkey. Damascus is the country's capital and the largest city. One interesting characteristic of this city was highlighted by one of the men I interviewed, "It is one of the oldest cities in the world."

Syrians are used to living in urban areas. Before the current war, most of the country's population was located in the towns. "Prior to the uprising, Syria's population was around 22 million, with more than half of the population formerly concentrated in urban centers."[13]

Although Islam represents the major faith expression in the country (90 percent of Syrians are Muslims), Syrian society is heavily multiethnic. Some of the people groups found in Syria are Arabs, Alawites, Bedouins, Palestinians, Kurds, and Turks. The most prominent religious groups are Muslims (Sunnis, Shias, and Druze), Christians (Protestant, Anglican, Catholic, and Orthodox), and Baha'i.

12. Lutheran Services Carolinas. "Refugee and Immigrant Services," para. 1.
13. Abboud, *Syria*, 19.

The Syrian refugees I interviewed belong to four families, each family with a minimum of five people. The largest family has a total of eleven members. Upon their arrival in Columbia, they were placed in two areas of the city: St. Andrews and downtown Columbia.

At the time the interviews were conducted, three of the four husbands had full-time jobs at different restaurants in Columbia and were working in order to support their families and become financially independent.

The following sections outline several characteristics of Syrian culture. Some of them, the Syrians have been able to maintain as they adjust to life in America; others, they are losing over time.

FAITH ASPECTS

All the Syrians assisted by the church identify themselves as Sunni Muslims. One fascinating aspect of the Syrian refugees' faith that I observed was that they don't publicly question God, even when they share about the loss of family members or the ongoing struggles in Syria. When the chemical gas attack happened in Khan Sheikhoun town on April 4, 2017, killing dozens of people, one of the wives expressed her sorrow with tears in her eyes, but she concluded using the expression *Alhamdulillah* in Arabic, which means, praise be to God.

When having to present a reason for the conflicts in their country, Syrians prefer to blame people instead of God: "The problem in Syria is that people have a bad heart," mentioned one of the husbands. He also criticized specifically people who belong to ISIS, "The ISIS fighters are not good people because they are not good Muslims. They are a shame to the Muslim people."

FAMILY STRUCTURE

Family is an essential part of life for Syrians. Sadly, all these refugees have in the United States is their nuclear family, since they have lost or left their extended family members.

For Syrians to remain unmarried is a sign of dishonor in their society, especially for women. Among other things, singleness can represent bad luck or even a curse, among other things. But, in their culture, to get married is not enough. Married couples must have children. "It is a disaster if a couple cannot have kids," said one of the wives. In Syrian society, a couple that can have many children are considered prosperous and blessed by God.

Marriage, in most cases, is arranged by families, and therefore contemporary dating is not accepted in the culture. Often, a wife will get to know her husband only a few months or weeks before the wedding. One of the couples I met got married after they had known each other for four months.

Usually, the fathers are responsible for finding a good spouse for their child to marry. There are, however, exceptions. In the case of one of the interviewed couples, it was the mother of the husband who arranged the marriage. He described, "My mother saw the girl, and liked her very much. Then, she arranged an opportunity for us to meet and I liked her as well. Our families met, discussed the wedding, and we got married."

The refugees I interviewed believe that love is not the most important characteristic in a marriage. "Many marriages fail because people marry based on love, not on commitment," said one of the participants. According to his perspective, when people marry based on love, and eventually think there is no more love; they divorce. He thinks the foundation of marriage should be a commitment, and love will flourish in the marriage as time goes by.

Among Syrians, it is also possible for marriages to occur among extended family members. One of the couples shared that they are cousins. "Our marriage was arranged by our family when I was very young," said the wife.

As Muslims, Syrian men are allowed to marry up to four wives.[14] However, all the Syrians who were interviewed had only one wife. They mentioned that there are Muslims in Columbia who have four wives and highlighted that each wife lives in a different house.

---

14. They base this practice on a verse in the Qur'an: Sura 4:4.

When discussing the possibility of their husbands having more than one wife, one lady said, "It is not good for the men to have four wives, but sometimes they need to. That is why they are allowed to have more than one, according to our religion."

One husband justified the need to marry more than one wife by pointing to two reasons: "If the first wife is sick or cannot have kids, then you can have other wives." Seemingly uncomfortable by what he said, his wife commented, "I would be very sad if he would marry another wife."

In relation to children, one traditional saying based on the hadiths (records of the traditions or sayings of the Prophet Muhammad)[15] was shared in one of the interviews, "If a child looks like the father, it is a sign that the wife loves the husband more than the husband loves the wife and vice versa."

COMMUNITY STRUCTURE

Syrians have a strong sense of community, but since they have been living as refugees for years, some of their family members are scattered in various countries, and others have died as a result of the war, they have lost their community structure, and the nuclear family is the only piece of the structure that remains.

During the interviews, refugees expressed how much they miss their family members. They described how their families are scattered in different places as a people group and mentioned that those still in Syria are facing mental problems (due to the war) and living in desperate circumstances. This emphasis on the extended family is a characteristic of their culture and seems deeper than the American sense of extended family.

One main obstacle to building a new community structure in Columbia is language. When they were asked, "How are your neighbors?" One responded, "I don't know. I cannot talk to them and build relationships."

Another obstacle that affects their lives in Columbia is transportation. One said, "Without a car, we depend on others to drive

15. See Bukhari, *Collection of Hadith*, 770–71.

us around. Therefore, we cannot easily go out and visit people in other neighborhoods."

Their identity as a people has been changing as they adjust to life in a new society and community structure. Little by little, they are walking away from their identity as Syrians and assimilating into an international culture. The kids, in particular, have become citizens of two worlds. One of them said, "I am not a Syrian anymore. Now I am an American. I lost my Arabic and just speak English." Naturally, this creates tension in the family, especially when the parents do not learn English. To watch their children losing their mother tongue and identifying with the host culture creates an especially painful dynamic.

CULTURAL ASPECTS

While the men vary in their appearance (hair, beard, clothes, and shoes), and some of the boys often dress like Americans, all the Syrian women in the group wear *abaya* (robe-like dress) and headscarf. One of the women explained that the abaya is a sign of faith and modesty. By covering their body and hair, they keep the men from looking and reserve the right to display their beauty just to their husbands. "Little girls do not need to wear *abaya* or headscarf. It is only when they enter puberty that they are required to do so," commented another woman. In their understanding, puberty is a sign that a girl is ready to get married.

Among the four families, two of them do not shake hands with people from a different gender. They have explained this behavior as a sign of respect. Touching a person from a different gender is considered a cultural expression of inappropriate intimacy and shameful behavior.

Shame and honor are among the most important concepts to Syrians. "How shameful!" is a commonly used expression when they disagree with a certain behavior that dishonors the people involved. Another reference to honor was made by one of the wives to express how she feels about Christians visiting her home, "The Christians are the ones who have been visiting our homes and drinking coffee with us. They always honor us with their visits."

COMMUNITY RELATIONSHIPS

More than one Syrian complained that the local Muslim community in Columbia had not embraced them. One wife affirmed that they received no support from the imam of the local mosque, not even when her husband was sick, "Muslims did not come to visit him. Only the Christians came."

The follow-up question focused on attempting to understand why other Muslims are staying away from Syrian refugees. They replied, suggesting that maybe this embarrassing situation happens because they are from Syria. My Syrian refugee friends think that people, in general, assume they are somehow related to ISIS. This is heartbreaking. After all that they have suffered, they still have to deal with the pain of rejection by the Muslim community and strive to assimilate into the broader community.

Then, talking about relationships in Columbia with non-Muslims, another husband said, "Americans are good people, especially the ones from the church. They treat us well and help us to feel at home."

Most of the Syrians assisted by the church now have access to a Christian church for the first time in their lives. The exile is resulting in an opportunity to build relationships with Christians and encounter the gospel of Jesus Christ.

EXAMPLES OF CHURCHES
REACHING OUT TO REFUGEES

Fortunately, there are many good examples of churches practicing God's word by serving refugees in different parts of the world. As a consequence, there are thousands of refugees who are finding shelter in the midst of their anguish and are coming to faith in Christ. Here are just a few examples:

Germany

Growing numbers of Muslim refugees in Germany meet weekly to worship Jesus at Trinity Church in Berlin. In an article called "Muslim Refugees Converting to Christianity in Berlin Church," published by the *The Christian Post*, Pastor Gottfried Martens reports some of what is going on in Germany. In a period of two years, his congregation grew from 150 to 700 members. The majority of this growth is due to Muslims from Iran and Afghanistan coming to faith in Christ. One of the converts, an Iranian called Mohammed Ali Zonoobi, who decided to become a Christian and be baptized, told the newspaper, "I feel like I am born again."[16]

United Kingdom

The number of refugees is growing in the United Kingdom as it is throughout Western Europe. Liverpool's Anglican Cathedral in the United Kingdom is trying to address the challenge. The congregation is working in partnership with the local authorities and with different organizations to reach out effectively.[17]

They have been engaging refugees from places like Syria, Eritrea, Iraq, Iran, Pakistan, and Somalia and are seeing some of them embracing the Christian faith. In an article published by *The Guardian,* we find a description of some of the activities the church develops with refugees: "At Liverpool's Anglican Cathedral in the UK, a weekly Persian service attracts between 100 and 140 people. Nearly all are migrants from Iran, Afghanistan, and elsewhere in Central Asia."[18]

16. Basilan, "Muslim Refugees Converting to Christianity in Berlin Church," para. 3.

17. See further Diocese of Liverpool, "Refugees—Responding with Heart and Mind."

18. Sherwood and Oltermann, "Growing Flock of Muslim Refugees are Converting," para. 6.

The Netherlands

A group of believers in Amsterdam, formed mainly by Brazilian immigrants, is working to reach out to Muslim refugees in the city. They serve in partnership with a church called *Comunidade Evangélica Vida Plena*.[19] They have been organizing bazaars to provide clothing for Syrian and Iraqi refugees living in Amsterdam. The group has decided not to give the clothes for free. Instead, the people involved in the refugee ministry charge about one euro per piece of clothing. Brother Jorge Ceni, the pastor of the church, says, "We sell the clothes to avoid the dependency idea in our relationship. We want to tell them that they are able to pay and buy. They are refugees, but they still can have something valuable to give in exchange. We think acting in this way we are helping them to uphold their dignity."[20]

The United States of America

Christians are engaging refugees in many communities across the United States and reaching out to the strangers in their midst. Churches, such as Kilbourne Park Baptist Church[21] and Hope Church[22] in Columbia, South Carolina, are reaching out to refugees. Also, Quest Church[23] in Seattle, Washington, and WoodsEdge Community Church[24] in Spring, Texas, maintain ministries reaching out to immigrants and refugees. In addition to churches, parachurch ministries reach out to populations of immigrants across the country. The Navigators have a ministry arm called "Nations Within" doing exactly that. They are active in cities where immigrants and refugees

19. See further Road of Hope's website, http://roadofhope.org.

20. Jorge Ceni, personal communication, April 24, 2016.

21. See further Kilbourne Park Baptist Church's website, www.kilbournepark.org.

22. See further Hope Church's website, https://hopechurchcola.org.

23. See further Quest Church's website, https://seattlequest.org.

24. See further WoodsEdge Community Church website, www.woodsedge.org.

have settled over the years. Appendix 4 provides a list of organizations dedicated to helping refugees, including Christian organizations.

It is exciting to see all the ways God is using his people to bless the lives of refugees and, at the same time, working through refugees to do something new in his church. In some parts of the world, but particularly in Europe, God is using refugees to bring revival to the local churches. As Sam George highlights, "I believe that one of the ways God is reviving Christianity in Europe is through refugees."[25] Therefore, the church is more than privileged to partake in God's marvelous work.

In light of how God's Spirit is moving on the face of the earth, I only wish that more Christians would embrace the task with which our great God has entrusted us: the message of reconciliation as Christ's ambassadors to the world. Paul states it beautifully in 2 Corinthians 5:18–20: "All this is from God, who reconciled us to himself through Christ and gave us the ministry of reconciliation: that God was reconciling the world to himself in Christ, not counting people's sins against them. And he has committed to us the message of reconciliation. We are therefore Christ's ambassadors, as though God were making his appeal through us."

---

25. See George and Adeney, *Refugee Diaspora*, 292.

DISCUSSION QUESTIONS

1. How significant is to better understand the refugees who live in our context?
2. As you read the Syrian views of life, what aspects stood out to you?
3. Why are the Syrian refugees having access to the gospel for the first time in the United States? What prevented them from hearing the gospel freely in Syria?
4. Why do you think the gospel is making an impact in the lives of refugees around the world?
5. How important is it for churches around the world to welcome the refugees in their contexts?

PRAY FOR THE REFUGEES

Pray for the victims of the refugee crisis, especially for the widows and orphans. Pray for those who are scattered in contexts where they are discriminated against and abused. Pray that they will be able to find comfort for their bodies, souls, and spirits to overcome the consequences of war, persecution, and natural disasters.

CALL TO ACTION

Talk to at least five friends about the challenges that refugees face in their attempt to escape from their dangerous living context and rebuild their lives in a strange land. Discuss with them some initiatives you can take together to assist the refugees in your area.

5

Back Story

Research for Deeper Understanding

We must never minimize the suffering of another.
Scripture's mandate to us is,
"Weep with them that weep" (Romans 12:15).

—BILLY GRAHAM

When the family woke up and sat down for breakfast together, they had no idea it would be the last meal they would share. Little did they know; the sun had just dawned on the worst day of their lives. Mere hours later, Leila lost her husband, Sayed, when military forces attacked their village in the Rakhine State of the Asian country of Myanmar.

Sayed was a civilian. He worked as a farmer and was loved by his community. Although he represented no violent threat, he was killed simply because he was a Rohingya. In his executors' eyes, he belonged to the "wrong" ethnic people group. By their estimation, he deserved nothing but death.

It was about noon when Sayed heard that his village was under attack. His concern was for his mother. She was a widow, lived alone, and suffered from diabetes, high cholesterol, and arrhythmia. Sayed knew that she could not defend herself or run away if the soldiers came.

Sayed left his wife and daughter at home and rushed to his mother's house to rescue her. In the streets, he grew increasingly terrified by the number of dead bodies he saw and the amount of smoke billowing from burned residences.

Tragically, when Sayed was just steps from his mother's front door, the soldiers arrived. They approached Sayed in a military vehicle and stopped a short distance away. Before he could even turn to look, they shot him in the back. From her kitchen window, in shocked horror, his mother witnessed his murder.

For several preceding years, Sayed had been considering leaving Myanmar. His people, the Rohingya, as a Muslim minority group, had been facing discrimination, religious persecution, and violence. His goal was to escape with his family and resume life in the neighboring country of Bangladesh. Sadly, the day Sayed finally decided to leave the country was the day he died. He did not manage to get out of his village with his loved ones. Instead, eight bullets tore through his body, causing massive damage to some of his vital organs.

Through a phone call, Leila heard what had happened to Sayed. She realized that a genocide attempt was going on and that she must act. She did not have time to mourn her husband or bury his body. Aware that troops were getting close and fearing to be captured, raped, or killed, Leila snatched up her two-year-old daughter, Nur, and fled. Mother and daughter joined a group of women and children who also decided to leave their village and sought refuge. Trying to hide from the military forces, they stole into a forest reserve. The brave group walked for three days before finally reaching the country's border. From there, they took a fishing boat to the Kutupalong Refugee Camp in Bangladesh.

Leila and Nur stayed at the camp for two years, living with hundreds of thousands of other refugees, all victims of similar inhumane crimes. Most of them were women and children, the two groups representing the majority of the world's refugees.

Life at Kutupalong was so hard that, at times, Leila felt tempted to return to her homeland. However, she kept resisting the idea of following her emotions. Rationally she knew that going back to Myanmar would represent, for Nur and herself, walking into the lion's den. Fortunately, the time came when they were approved for resettlement and were able to settle in Canada.

Today, mother and daughter are battling the traumas they have experienced. Although they still miss Sayed tremendously, they can put a smile on their faces. Leila and Nur are happy to live in a context where there is a real opportunity for them to overcome their bad memories and build a new future. Will they find people willing to come alongside and help them experience a new life? Will Leila and Nur find a church with arms wide open to welcome them as part of the family?

In this chapter, we will begin to analyze a case study based on the refugee ministry developed by Arsenal Hill Presbyterian Church.

This research focuses on accessing and evaluating the ministry practices carried out by the AHPC using as a frame of reference the twenty-three principles outlined on the *Best Practices for Christian Ministry Among Forcibly Displaced People* document by the Refugee Highway Partnership.[1]

The comparative analysis's primary goal is to identify areas of strength and weakness in the refugee ministry and extract lessons that can enhance the work. Hopefully, the overall learning experience will also benefit the reader who wants to replicate best practices in the engagement of refugees in any given context.

The Refugee Highway Partnership document covers areas related to three specific groups: *church volunteers*, *resettlement agency personnel*, and *refugees*. To conduct my study, I interviewed and collected data from people represented by the three groups in an attempt to listen to their perspectives and deepen my understanding of the significance of the refugee ministry.

As we examine the interviewees' answers, we notice that each voice embodies different aspects of the work and points to how God is working through the refugee ministry. If you miss any, you miss

---

1. See further RHP, "Best Practices for Christian Ministry."

the full picture. Although your local context may vary, consider what you may learn from this particular case study so that it may be applied in your own interactions or ministry with refugees.

The details of the questionnaire and research methodology are described in Appendix 1 and Appendix 2. Next, I present the questions that were asked during the interviews and the respective answers given by the individuals representing the three groups. The questions are tagged with the name of each specific group along the sections. In this way, the reader will be able to contextualize the answers. For the sake of confidentiality, names have been omitted to render individuals unidentifiable.

SECTION 1: MINISTRY POLICY AND PRACTICE

Question 1 (Church volunteers): Regarding the people involved in the refugee ministry, what are the signs of their relationship with God and other people?

"A majority of the volunteers are committed believers in Christ who are involved in local churches. One or two are not believers, though they have volunteered to help because of their compassion and their relationship with other volunteers. Many of the volunteers have gone out of their way to visit and build deeper relationships with the refugee families."

"The love of Christ is very evident in all of our volunteers. It is this selfless aspect of service in Jesus's name that speaks louder than any other of the volunteers' relationship with God. This God-like quality is not only evidenced in the consistent, unpaid service each one renders but in the cheerful and flexible availability I see in each person. It has been a deep source of joy for me to witness people who had little to no meaningful contact with Muslims before having such an involvement in the ministry now. I feel encouraged to see how the volunteers love our Muslim friends, especially in the social, cultural, and political situation we find ourselves in America today."

Question 2 (Refugees): Do you feel affirmed by the church in your dignity and value?

"The people from AHPC are very nice. Since we got here, they have been helping us very much. I thank God for them, and I am happy to come here. I feel loved and cared for by them. Also, I like it when we have special events, and I am asked to bring food to share. They always show appreciation for the food I bring."

"Yes! The Christians here value and love us. On Sundays, we feel happy when we wake up because it is the day my children and I come to church. The Christians that I know are very gentle. They are my family here in America."

Question 3 (Refugees): Is the church assisting you in response to your needs without discrimination?

"The church is teaching us, visiting us, and praying for us. There is no discrimination on their side. They treat us as equal people. Here, there are no Muslims or Christians. We are just one people."

"Yes, they are assisting me, and there is no discrimination. I feel at home when I am here. They value us as people and are even trying to learn our language. When we had our last event, I was overwhelmed with joy to see they had built for us a mudhif.[2] They had all the Arab objects in there just as we have at home, and I felt I was in my country. They show love and respect for us."

Question 4 (Church volunteers): Are you developing your ministry strategies based on sound research and assessment? If not, on what are you basing your ministry strategies?

"This is an area for definite improvement. We entered into this ministry less than three months after beginning a revitalization of our church as a church plant, so research and assessment were not

2. A reed house or coffee house traditionally built by the Marsh Arabs in the swamps of southern Iraq. Mudhifs are usually used for dwellings and for meeting places. They carry a lot of symbolism for Iraqis, even for the ones who are not from the marsh areas.

given much priority. Essentially, our initiative and motivation for this ministry were born out of the necessity of alleviating some of the pressure of the Kilbourne Park Baptist Church, which had become overwhelmed by its ESL student numbers. Before beginning, we met to plan our ESL ministry program and received help and training from an experienced ESL teacher and teacher trainer, as well as helpful suggestions and overall program design from one of our members who is trained in TESOL. Revisiting things like sound research and assessment would definitely help to make our ministry more effective."

"We are basing our ministry strategies mostly on the cross-cultural experiences and the ESL teaching experiences of several of our volunteers. Moreover, we have had some basic training from Lutheran Services Carolinas, and a TESOL professor from Columbia International University, Tina Winchester Walker. A few of our volunteers are currently taking classes related to diaspora ministry and ESL, which informs their teaching and involvement with our refugee students."

Question 5 (Church volunteers): How effective and honest do you think your communication with the refugees is?

"We have had to rely heavily on our church members who are proficient in the Arabic language for communicating with our Arabic-speaking refugee friends about logistics, such as transportation, and scheduling. This has been effective. We are growing in our communication with the refugees and have adopted basic communication strategies that have been helpful. Overall, our communication with the refugees is based on honesty."

"I believe our communication with our refugee friends is constantly growing in effectiveness and honesty. The language barrier is still an issue with most volunteers and students for deep communication, but at the same time, much is communicated without words, but through loving each other and being involved in each other's life. One good example of communication is when a high school refugee expressed to her ESL conversation partners that she is not taking any science classes at school and wants to be able to take science classes. We still haven't resolved this issue, but I thought it was a good example of open, honest communication between volunteers and refugee students."

Question 6 (Church volunteers): Do you see your group (people involved in the refugee ministry) as a learning entity?

"Yes. In addition to learning from people with refugee ministry experience and ESL experience, we also seek to learn from each other and learn and build on our experiences up to this point. We meet periodically to debrief and to plan for the next stages of ministry."

"Yes, I definitely see our group as a learning entity. Most of us are new to refugee ministry and have learned tremendously since we began. We have provided some limited cultural education related to Muslims, which I believe has been helpful. I believe that biblical theology to form a stronger foundation for our purpose in fulfilling the LORD's calling as the one who is the LORD of the sojourner and wanderer would support our ministry in new and powerful ways."

SECTION 2: THE ROLE OF ADVOCACY

Question 7 (Church volunteers): How motivated are you for advocacy on behalf of the refugees?

"I think our volunteers are very motivated to be advocates for refugees. The genuine relationships that have developed have helped our volunteers to see refugees as people just like them. We should probably do more to advocate for refugees in the political realm as we see that the United States is taking in an incredibly low number of refugees this year, which is especially sad when the number of refugees in the world is at the highest level ever!"

"We would love to invest more time in broader support and advocacy for refugees. We have attended a rally at the capital supporting immigrants and refugees. Although we would love to invest more time in advocacy on behalf of refugees with political leaders, we do feel strongly that our most effective advocacy comes from having thirty volunteers involved in the program who are building relationships with refugees. These volunteers are sharing stories of their refugee friends with their neighbors, co-workers, and fellow students."

Question 8 (Church volunteers): How do you do advocacy on behalf of the refugees in the public square and within the Christian community? Is it grace-based, honest, and performed with integrity?

"I attended a South Carolina Senate Subcommittee Meeting, where community representatives debated specific bills related to refugee resettlement. I have also written to State representatives, stating the benefits of continued refugee resettlement and guaranteeing our welcome and embracing of refugee families to ensure that they are better integrated into our society and culture. Yes, I believe our advocacy is grace-based, honest, and performed with integrity. As a church, we seek to be an example to the Christian community and in the public square of how a small church, with thirty-five active members currently, and with very limited resources, is able to reach out in grace to a significant number of refugees. We have been approached by a non-Christian University of South Carolina student who is interested in bringing members of her class to assist in our program."

"We advocate for refugees by encouraging other churches in our denomination and other churches in our city to be involved in ministry to refugees as well. As a small church, we can honestly say, 'If we can do it, you can do it.' Additionally, we try to get accurate information about refugees to our family, friends, and other contacts. One of the best ways to do this is to share the stories of the refugees that we have gotten to know."

Question 9 (Church volunteers): Are you working in collaboration with refugees and other advocacy groups?

"We are working in collaboration with Lutheran Services Carolinas and with the refugee ministry coordinator for our denomination."

"Our ministry began through consultation with LSC, through whom we received our contact with the refugee families who are now our ESL students and friends, and we maintain occasional contact with them about the ministry and the refugee families."

SECTION 3: THE ROLE OF THE CHURCH

Question 10 (Church volunteers): What is the role of the church concerning the refugee ministry?

"The church plays a critical role in the refugee ministry by providing prayer support, publicity through announcements during our worship services, facilities, resources, recruitment, volunteer mechanisms, and leadership. Many of the volunteers themselves, in turn, invest their own time, resources, and vehicles in providing the teaching, transportation, etc., for the ministry. The pastor and his family are fully involved in the ministry."

"Our role as a church is primarily to provide quality weekly ESL lessons. Furthermore, we have mobilized teachers involved in the weekly ESL lessons to serve as tutors for refugee families and individuals. We are also involved in home visits and organizing activities (dinners, sporting events, baby showers) with the goal of building friendships with our refugee neighbors. The overarching role is to welcome these refugees into the city and convey to them that we are happy that they are in Columbia."

Question 11 (Church volunteers): What are the external resources the church is utilizing in the refugee ministry?

"The church is utilizing time and skills provided by a significant number of volunteers who do not attend the church. Besides, it is also utilizing the facilities and finances provided by members and non-members through donated use of a property for hospitality and on occasion through financial donations."

"The church has been recruiting volunteers from CIU and USC. We try to recruit Christians who have similar values, are willing to love the refugees, and have the passion for sharing the gospel. Through the volunteers from our congregation and outside of the congregation, we are able to help the refugees to a broader extent, so that they learn the language, understand the local culture, and are introduced into life in the city. We are happy to help the refugees in a variety of practical ways, such as providing transportation, contacting doctors and dentists, offering translation in interviews, and making appointments because we count on the help of external resources too."

SECTION 4: THE ROLE OF REFUGEES

Question 12 (Church volunteers): Are the refugees involved as partners in the ministry? How?

"The refugees are involved as partners in the ministry to the degree that some of them who are more proficient in English assist us in communicating logistics information throughout the community of refugees we are serving. They are also partnering in the sense that they contribute to potluck meal gatherings."

"We are finding new ways to include them in planning new events. For example, the refugee families brought food to our recent potluck. This was a way for them to share their culture with us."

SECTION 5: THE ROLE OF ORGANIZATIONS

Question 13 (Church volunteers): What are the agencies that are assisting the church in accomplishing the vision and mission of the refugee ministry?

"Lutheran Services Carolinas is assisting the church through providing education, contact with refugees, and through helpful advice and counsel. World Witness and Outreach North America are

assisting the church through prayer and through generating awareness within the Associate Reformed Presbyterian Church denomination about our refugee ministry and more broadly about refugee
ministry in general."

"The LSC. Students and professors/administrators from CIU.
Undergraduate and graduate students from the USC. A Christian
organization called A Moment of Hope."

Question 14 (Resettlement agency): How are you empowering local churches in refugee ministry?

"LSC empowers churches to be involved in refugee ministry
through education and training. LSC partners with churches and
regularly meets with them to share our mission and vision to serve
refugee families in the Midlands and Charleston areas. Interested
churches are encouraged to offer support and services to refugee
families and/or to be matched directly with a newly arrived family
to walk with the new family through the resettlement process. LSC
acts as support and guidance to churches as they embark in their
refugee ministry."

Question 15 (Resettlement agency): Is your agency utilizing resources beyond your own and are cooperating with other groups?

"LSC utilizes resources beyond our own and cooperates with
churches and other organizations. LSC will provide referrals to other agencies and groups that may be able to assist with the refugee
community for any service that we are unable to provide. We work
closely with many other organizations that offer ESL classes, orientation classes, assistance with transportation, financial assistance,
etc. Besides, LSC utilizes resources that local churches are willing
to provide to refugee families in need."

Question 16 (Resettlement agency): How is your agency networking with other ministries along the "highway"?

"LSC networks with other ministries that serve refugees and provides referrals to our clients when they have a need that the ministry can meet. LSC is always looking for new ministries that can assist in meeting the needs of the refugee community. LSC realizes that it takes the community working together to ensure that refugees are well cared for and welcome in their new community. Ministries and churches are essential to the work that we do."

Question 17 (Resettlement agency): Is your agency seeking to resource your ministries from your host country's economy?

"LSC Refugee Services is funded through the federal government since that is where our contracts come from in order to provide services to refugees. We also receive private donations from churches and individuals that are all located in the United States. LSC does not seek out resources from ministries outside our host country."

SECTION 6: MINISTRY CONTEXT

Question 18 (Church volunteers): Is any organization collaborating appropriately with the church, giving careful consideration to the regional, cultural, political, and historical context? How is it happening?

"Our denomination's foreign missions' agency and our national based organization focused on developing relationships with our Muslim neighbors are supportive of our efforts, providing counsel, prayer, financial, and staff support. LSC is helping us in this regard as well, and its director has given orientation and training to our volunteers in one of our debriefing meetings."

"I know we are receiving this kind of collaboration. But, I am not sure what are the organizations involved. When we have a debriefing meeting, we always have someone who comes to speak to us and share helpful insights. Last time we had a representative from an organization called A Moment of Hope sharing how abortion is affecting the Congolese refugees in Columbia."

Question 19 (Church volunteers): Is the ministry flexible, innovative, and creative in responding to changing conditions along the Refugee Highway?

"We were providentially able to respond to a significant change in the refugee landscape in Columbia by being ready to specifically minister to a large group of Syrian refugees who had newly arrived in Columbia. As we have developed relationships with our students over the past year and a half, we are more aware of their needs, and they are more open to sharing with us. Because most of them have come through traumatic situations, we are praying and seeking to develop a program to offer counseling. This is in the very early stages of research as we talk with area hospitals and professional counselors in the area."

"We are recognizing the need to be flexible, as some of the refugee families have recently moved locally, requiring changes in our transportation routes for ESL class pickups. We also recognize the need to network more on a national basis, given the reality that some of the refugee families find greater opportunities in other states and so have begun to move out of our area. We have also added two new families within the past few months, both from Congo. Innovation and creativity could be emphasized more in our ministry."

Question 20 (Church volunteers): How well do you understand your local context? Are you aware of potential risks and crises in your specific ministry context?

"The Muslim refugee community has received some financial assistance from area mosques, although the refugee families attest to the fact that only Christians are visiting them in their homes and maintaining a significant relationship with them. One crisis that has developed from mosque assistance is a strong sense of favoritism, inequality, and abuse of donated funds, resulting in jealousy, resentment, and even in some families moving or attempting to move out of our area. We are aware that the environment within which we are working is a sensitive one. Perhaps we need to be more prayerful about how to proceed in this context, even concerning communication with the Muslim community."

"As volunteers, before we sign up for the work, we are required to read a Cultural Sensitivity Document (see Appendix 3) so that we can learn about important customs and aspects of the Muslim culture represented by our international friends. This document is an important resource the church uses to avoid misunderstandings in our ministry context and to maintain a good relationship with our students."

SECTION 7: PARTNERSHIP

Question 21 (Church volunteers): Are partnerships happening in your refugee ministry? With whom? In which areas?

"We have partnerships with area churches and with CIU and USC students. A local Middle Eastern restaurant called Al-Amir has provided discounted authentic halal meals for our ESL dinners. Besides, refugees from the local mosque have invited ESL teachers to attend special events at the local mosque."

"Yes, partnerships are happening between our church and non-member volunteers, as well as with CIU. We have been able to help meet requirements for CIU students attending their Christian Service Learning program."

Question 22 (Church volunteers): What are the meaningful perspectives and gifts your partners are bringing to the process?

"We have a good number of volunteers with experience in Muslim majority countries. This perspective helps structure the program and educate volunteers who do not have this experience. Many of our volunteers have teaching gifts. Many of our volunteers have the gift of friendship. I think one of the most valuable aspects of our ministry is the number of volunteers who have visited the homes of refugees and eaten together and laughed together and done their best to communicate."

"Both CIU and USC students are bringing training in TESOL to our process and ministry. Younger students bring energy and relatability with our younger refugee student friends, such as one young CIU student who took four of our middle school boy refugee friends to a soccer game at CIU and has taken them there to play soccer as well. Our older, more experienced volunteers connected with CIU and Ben Lippen School offer great insight, wisdom, and suggestions that have been integrated into our ministry on occasion with good results. Our church members themselves provide a variety of gifts and skills, including hospitality, leadership, giftedness in working with children, a healthy emphasis on relational outreach and friendship, abilities in teaching, recruiting new volunteers, and prayer."

Question 23 (Church volunteers): What are some of the examples of shared work, risk, responsibility, accountability, decision-making, and benefits concerning your partners?

"Recently, a member of another church introduced us to an Iraqi family who cannot attend our weekly Sunday ESL meetings and would like ESL lessons during the week. We were able to mobilize one of our ESL volunteers to meet with them weekly at their home. As we work with a wide range of volunteers, we need to constantly be mindful that many of the volunteers do not have a cross-cultural experience. For example, we have to educate our volunteers regarding appropriate dress and male/female relationship boundaries. We have debriefing and planning meetings periodically and provide opportunities for volunteers to give feedback and suggestions."

"Logistics, especially transportation, is a clear example of work shared by our partners and could be considered shared risk since individual drivers are transporting refugees in their own vehicles and under their own insurance policies. Shared responsibility is seen in the care of refugee children and youth, as the parents entrust their children to our care and teaching, without an awareness of what is occurring or being taught within the classes. Accountability is provided partly through multiple individuals being present in each teaching and childcare situation. Decision-making is shared through follow-up and planning meetings following each ESL term. The benefits are great and varied. They include the opportunity for believers to partner together in unity and to increasingly take part in the growing community of people, churches, and organizations serving refugees in our area. Benefits include the opportunity to enfold new volunteers who attend our church and become members in some cases. It is also a benefit to university students majoring or minoring in TESOL to have a ministry and program to plug into in order to gain experience in teaching English. Besides, some missionaries, either on home assignment or now settled in our area, have benefited from the ministry and service opportunity provided through our refugee ministry, giving them an outlet to use their gifts, training, and experience, and to fulfill their missionary passion."

VOICES AND NEEDS

The voices and needs shared in this chapter of people like Leila and Nur, and of many others who were part of the interviews, may be in a location far from you. Nevertheless, as you look around in your context, you may find similar voices and needs. God has allowed displaced people to come to you as part of a divine purpose. He is the one permitting the movements of people across the globe to fulfill a greater plan. As J. D. Payne points out, "the movements of peoples across the globe are a part of the outworking of the LORD's plan leading to the day when his kingdom will come."[3]

As a result of all the suffering they have undergone, the refugees around you may be feeling "harassed and helpless, like sheep without a shepherd" (Matt 9:36), and in need of your specific help.

Remember, God wants to be glorified in the lives of the refugees through the divine light he has placed in you: "let your light

3. Payne, *Strangers Next Door*, 32.

shine before others, that they may see your good deeds and glorify your Father in heaven" (Matt 5:16).

Will you offer your life to be part of the solution to this global crisis? Will you take an action today and make an impact in the lives of the displaced ones? Will you make good use of the extraordinary opportunity God is giving you to welcome, serve, and share the gospel with the refugees in your midst?

DISCUSSION QUESTIONS

1. What is the relevance of listening to all the groups involved in serving in a refugee ministry?
2. Which quote from the interviews spoke most to you? Why was this significant to you?
3. If you had the chance to conduct the interviews, what questions would you add to the questionnaire?
4. Based on the answers to the research questions, what are your impressions about the work being carried by the AHPC?
5. What is God speaking to you at this point? How will you respond? List specific action points.

PRAY FOR THE REFUGEES

Pray for the countries hosting the largest numbers of refugees that they will be able to offer the support the refugees need. Pray for Turkey, Lebanon, and Jordan to continue to embrace the refugees. Pray for other nations around the world to open their borders and welcome the refugees as well.

CALL TO ACTION

Make a commitment to pray regularly for the refugees living in your city. Ask God to direct you to strategic places where you can meet refugees and build meaningful relationships with the ones living in proximity to you.

6

Improving Your Story

Evaluation and Best Practices

*Christian living moves from what God has freely done
for us in Christ to what we should freely do for others.*

—John Piper

On my first trip to Mafraq, the closest Jordanian city to Zaatari
Refugee Camp, I met Samir, a twenty-year-old man from the
city of Homs in Syria. In a conversation with Abu Mohammed, his
father, I learned that Samir suffers from psychological problems
(probably PTSD) as a result of watching the Syrian civil war when
he was just a young boy. Abu Mohammed narrated how Samir was
always filled with dread as bombs were dumped over their city. The
boy knew the explosives were powerful, not just because of the terrifying sounds of their blasts, but because each rain of bombs left
behind bodies. In the short span of six months, he had lost three
uncles, each loss accompanied by noisy airplanes. Today, though
fully grown, Samir does not enjoy the full blessing of maturing into
adulthood. Instead, he lives in depressed isolation.

Imagine. Refugees like Abu Mohammed and Samir are accepted into a resettlement process. They travel hundreds of miles

with other family members, and they arrive in your country. They initiate life in a new society while carrying great suffering. They deal with extensive trauma, and now feel completely unsettled. Their high expectations are wed to high anxieties. They grapple with an entirely new living context with no idea how to overcome cultural, social, religious, and linguistic challenges. Our friends know they are lucky for having been relocated in a safe environment, but they have no idea that a new battle has just begun. They now have to rent a house, find a job, place their children in school, and so much more. Everything, including all the necessary paperwork, must be done in a language that they do not speak. Add to that how devasted they will feel if they are mistreated, discriminated against, or rejected in their new society.

It does not have to be so grim. God is calling us to welcome these refugees. He desires we build meaningful relationships with them and help them in everyday life, facilitating their resettlement process, which would be daunting regardless of the additional challenges they have already experienced.

FACTORS CONTRIBUTING TO THE MIGRATION CRISIS

Millions of individuals are forcibly displaced worldwide, including internally displaced people, refugees, and asylum seekers. A number of factors contribute to this chaotic scenario.

- Civil war as in Syria
- Oppressive regime as in Venezuela
- Violent extremism as in Afghanistan
- Food insecurity as in South Sudan
- Armed conflict as in Myanmar
- Islamist insurgency as in Somalia
- Dispute over land and leadership as in the Democratic Republic of Congo

- Ongoing violence as in the Central African Republic
- Religious, ethnic and political conflicts as in Nigeria
- Sectarian tensions as in Yemen

THE EUROPEAN RESPONSE TO THE CRISIS

Europe has been hugely affected by the current refugee crisis. The influx of refugees in Europe is so massive that it has been classified the European migrant crisis. In 2015, the United Nations estimated that eight thousand refugees were arriving in Europe every day.[1]

Refugees from the Middle East and North Africa manage to reach Europe primarily by paying sums of money to ruthless human traffickers. They send refugees across the Mediterranean in boats and rafts in a hazardous exile.

Getting to Europe is not a guarantee that refugees are going to find safety, protection, and shelter. UNHCR is aware of the dilemma and brings attention to the risks involving refugees who reach Europe: "These risks do not end once in Europe. Those moving onwards irregularly have reported numerous types of abuse, including being pushed back across borders."[2]

Human traffickers have used two primary routes through the Mediterranean Sea to smuggle refugees into Europe: 1) The Eastern Mediterranean (from Turkey to Greece) and 2) the Central Mediterranean (from North Africa to Italy and Malta). Both routes are extremely dangerous. The International Organization for Migration reports frequent shipwrecks involving refugees who die in their attempt to escape from war, violence, persecution, and other human rights violations to cross the Mediterranean.[3] The story of Alan and his family narrated in chapter 1 illustrates very well the dangers of these routes.

1. See "Europe Gets 8,000 Refugees Daily."
2. UNHCR, "Europe Situation," para. 2.
3. See further International Organization for Migration, "Mediterranean Migrant Arrivals."

Although refugees enter Europe mostly through Greece, Italy, and Malta, many of them do not stay in these countries. They usually look for the European countries where they can access the best opportunities to rebuild their lives. Many displaced people wish to settle in Germany because the country has opened its borders to welcome refugees and has a strong economy (among the world's top five). Nevertheless, reaching Germany is not an easy task. To do so, refugees must first cross other European countries that sometimes close their borders and do not allow them access. In many cases, they are deported or sent to detention centers or refugee camps.

THE MIDDLE EASTERN RESPONSE TO THE CRISIS

The Middle East is directly connected to the current refugee crisis. As we turn our eyes to the region, we find two meaningful realities. Firstly, Syria, the country *sending out* the most refugees to the world (over six million), is part of the region. Secondly, Turkey, the country that *hosts* the largest number of refugees in the world (nearly four million), is part of the region as well.

Also, when we consider the countries hosting the highest numbers of refugees worldwide compared to their native populations, we find three Middle Eastern countries at the top of the list: Lebanon, Jordan, and Turkey. "Lebanon hosts the largest number of refugees relative to its national population, where 1 in 6 people was a refugee. Jordan (1 in 11) and Turkey (1 in 28) ranked second and third, respectively."[4]

The contribution given by these three countries to the refugee crisis is remarkable; especially considering that Lebanon and Jordan as such small countries are still taking in an enormous number of refugees. And they are not only hosting refugees at camps, but also hosting refugees in most of their cities. For instance, in Jordan, 84 percent of Syrian refugees live outside of the refugee camps, mostly in urban areas, directly among Jordanians.[5]

---

4. UNHCR, "Global Trends: 2018," 3.
5. Reliefweb, "UNHCR Jordan Factsheet, May 2019," paras. 1–3.

Middle Eastern countries are doing their best to respond to the refugee crisis, but some are feeling overwhelmed and hoping that other nations will also make great efforts to follow their example.

THE GULF COUNTRIES RESPONSE TO THE CRISIS

The Gulf countries are not responding to the current refugee crisis by opening their borders to refugees. This is a surprise to the world since they seem uniquely positioned to do so: they are Muslims, they speak Arabic, and they are wealthy. Amnesty International has mentioned this lack of engagement in a report published in 2014, "The six Gulf countries—Qatar, United Arab Emirates, Saudi Arabia, Kuwait, and Bahrain—have offered zero resettlement places to Syrian refugees."[6]

The Syrian and Iraqi refugees in Columbia, South Carolina, have expressed disappointment regarding their fellow Muslims from the Gulf countries. One of them stressed in a conversation, "The Gulf countries did not receive any refugees while the United States and Europe received plenty of them. Even Israel helped with the wounded. I am amazed that our Arab brothers are not helping us."

The Gulf countries are willing to donate money to the refugee cause but not to welcome the refugees into their lands. The Syrians and Iraqis whom they usually host are individuals who have work and student visas, but not the refugees who need shelter the most.

Although hospitality is considered to be a high value in the cultures represented by the Gulf countries, they are closed societies that do not like cultural interferences or changes. Syrian refugees have indicated to me that this is a significant reason why the governments from the Gulf countries are not willing to receive huge numbers of refugees, regardless if they are Muslims.

6. Amnesty International, "Syria Refugee Crisis," para. 14.

THE UNITED STATES RESPONSE TO THE CRISIS

In line with the Geneva Convention, the United States has historically followed the principle of protecting and welcoming refugees.
Resettlement numbers in the country since 1975 are impressive,
according to UNHCR figures, and must be acknowledged: "The
United States has an exceptional history of welcoming refugees.
Since 1975, the United States has welcomed over 3 million refugees
for resettlement from all over the world, and with help from American families and communities, these refugees have now built new
lives and homes in all 50 states."[7]

The average number of refugees coming to the United States
has always varied year by year, as the numbers from the *Pew Research Center* point out: "From fiscal years 1990 to 1995, an average
of about 116,000 refugees arrived in the U.S. each year, with many
coming from the former Soviet Union. However, refugee admissions dropped off to roughly 27,100 in fiscal 2002 . . . following the
terrorist attacks in 2001."[8]

In 2016, the number of refugees officially accepted into the
country was 94,837, as reported by the Refugee Processing Center.[9] An article published in *Washington Week* lists the top countries that were allowed to send their refugees to America in that
year: "The Democratic Republic of the Congo contributed the
highest number of refugees last year at 16,370. Syria was second,
with 12,587 refugees from the war-torn nation entering the U.S.,
followed by Burma, Iraq and Somalia."[10]

In 2017, a significant change affected the national resettlement
program. The Trump administration decided to set a refugee limit
of 50,000 people per year to enter the United States. In that year,
this limit was reached in July 12, and only refugees who were able to
"prove close familial relationships to people that are already in the
country" were allowed to come to America.[11]

7. UNHCR, "This Land Is Your Land," para. 2.

8. Krogstad, "Key Facts About Refugees to the U.S.," para. 7.

9. See further Refugee Processing Center, "Interactive Reporting."

10. Greve, "Refugees in America: By the Numbers," para. 4.

11. Atwood, "U.S. Hits Refugee Limit for 2017," para. 4.

In recent years, there is an ongoing debate in the country related to the national refugee resettlement program. How many refugees should be admitted annually in the United States? On one side, people who want a lower number of resettlement admissions claim, for example, that some refugees are willingly putting themselves in a vulnerable position to get the chance to immigrate. On the contrary, those who are in favor of a higher number of refugee resettlements argue that welcoming refugees reinforces American values of justice, freedom, and generosity.

As a Brazilian, I do not feel qualified to defend one side or the other on the resettlement debate in the United States. Though I do hold opinions, it is up to American society to decide the course of the nation. So, I prefer to leave the discussion of this matter to the democratic process in the United States. My goal as I approach this issue is not to recommend specific political policies but to remind people who fear God that he loves the foreigner. As a consequence, the Almighty requires we meet the needs of those who are sojourners in our midst and treat them well.

EVALUATING THE REFUGEE MINISTRY AT ARSENAL HILL PRESBYTERIAN CHURCH

I understand that evaluation is one of the essential aspects of the development of any Christian ministry. We must be willing to evaluate the work with open hearts to listen, ponder, and learn. Openness to evaluation and improvement can only enhance the ministry's impact over time and allow for necessary change.

Responding to the current migration crisis is so important. Therefore, it is worth investing the time in thoughtful evaluation so that we can better posture ourselves for the future. And we must pursue it because we are called to do God's work diligently, instead of negligently: "A curse on anyone who is lax in doing the Lord's work!" (Jer 48:10).

The interviews conducted on the refugee ministry at Arsenal Hill Presbyterian Church provide a snapshot of the ministry at a specific point in time. Such a snapshot can be encouraging to those involved in the ministry, as it postulates feedback, adding value to the hours invested in serving refugees. In addition to providing information about the ministry, feedback is also important in assessing how the ministry can improve by better meeting the needs of the refugees.

The answers collected during the interviews and presented in the previous chapter showed that the Arsenal Hill Presbyterian Church is covering all the twenty-three principles based on the *Best Practices for Christian Ministry Among Forcibly Displaced People* proposed by the RHP. The numbering in the following sections is based on the principles detailed by RHP. The complete list is in Appendix 2.

The research has shown that in some areas, the AHPC is doing well; but in other areas, the church can improve services offered to the refugees. Hopefully, the following evaluation will inspire individual Christians and churches to take similar initiatives.

AREAS IN WHICH THE CHURCH IS DOING WELL

Section 1: Ministry Policy and Practice

Principle 1: Effective refugee ministry has relationship with God and people at its core.

The church intentionally seeks volunteers who know the LORD and want to make him known to the refugees. As a consequence, signs of relationship with God and people are primary characteristics visible among the volunteers who are serving the refugees. These signs are shown in areas such as prayer, fellowship, and gospel proclamation.

Principle 2: Refugees receive affirmation of their dignity, value, and the contribution they make.

The refugees are feeling affirmed by the church in their dignity and value. Besides approval, they show excitement in their descriptions of their relationship with the church. They feel appreciated when church members visit their homes and when they share their traditional food at the church's events.

*Principle 3: Organizations and churches assist refugees
in response to their needs without discrimination.*

They feel accepted and loved by the church. They do not point out any sign of discrimination in the relationship with the volunteers. They recognize and appreciate the efforts of church members to respect and value their culture.

Principle 6: Effective refugee ministries are learning entities.

Volunteers are aware that they are continually learning as they progress in the development of the refugee ministry. Also, volunteers are improving the services they provide as they learn more about the refugees' needs and acquire more knowledge and experience.

Section 2: The Role of Advocacy

*Principle 7: The motivation for advocacy is
for the benefit of those represented.*

There is a high level of motivation for advocacy on behalf of the refugees. One of the results of this feeling has been the recruitment of more volunteers as church members share with more and more people about their work. The answers showed, though, that the motivation should be translated into actions, especially in the public square.

Section 3: The Role of the Church

*Principle 10: The local church plays a vital
role in the ministry to refugees.*

Even though volunteers from outside of the church have been a great help in the work, it is primarily church members who are the most highly involved in the refugee ministry. These include the pastor and his family, which is admirable since the ESL classes happen on Sundays (when the pastoral families are very busy). The church provides its facilities, members, and other resources for the work to happen.

Principle 11: Local churches will utilize appropriate external resources for effective refugee ministry.

The volunteers from CIU and USC, for example, illustrate the external resources that the church is coopting in the development of refugee ministry. The church recognizes that it is unmanageable to do the work alone and has been recruiting and partnering with qualified volunteers to run the ministry.

Section 5: The Role of Organizations

Principle 13: Agencies are assisting refugee churches in accomplishing their vision and mission.

The church receives assistance from agencies to accomplish the vision and mission of the refugee ministry. The main agency is Lutheran Service Carolinas, which is the organization that connects the refugees to the church. There are others like A Moment of Hope and Outreach North America, as the survey has shown.

Principle 14: Agencies are empowering local host country churches in refugee ministry.

Besides connecting refugees to local churches (and other organizations in general), the LSC empowers the churches, offering them education, training, and accountability as they work together in the resettlement process of the refugee families.

*Principle 15: Agencies utilize resources beyond their
own and are cooperating with other groups.*

LSC is connected to other agencies and organizations that cover needed services they cannot fully provide. The partnership they have with churches like the AHPC to assist refugees is a form of cooperation between the agency and other institutions.

*Principle 16: Agencies are networking with
other ministries along the "highway."*

LSC heavily networks with other ministries. They are aware they need the help and the expertise of other ministries to fulfill their mission. Thus, they are always looking for groups with whom they can network.

*Principle 17: Agencies seek to resource their
ministries from host country economies.*

LSC is focused on seeking out resources for their ministries only from the host country. All their projects are funded by resources from the local (federal) government or from churches and individuals based in the United States.

Section 6: Ministry Context

*Principle 18: Refugee organizations collaborate appropriately
with the church, giving careful consideration to the
regional, cultural, political, and historical context.*

LSC, the resettlement agency, is the refugee organization collaborating and providing regional, cultural, political, and historical context in terms of refugee ministry.

LSC has been a crucial partner in the refugee ministry. They have supported the refugee ministry at AHPC in different areas, including orientation and training.

Principle 19: Ministries are flexible, innovative, and creative in responding to changing conditions along the Refugee Highway.

The refugee ministry at AHPC has been flexible, innovative, and creative. The church has been focusing on the needs of the refugees and making efforts to address them. One example is the effort to develop a counseling program to serve the refugees who need help overcoming trauma.

Principle 20: The local context will be understood in order to inform and influence all ministry activity.

The answers showed that the church members are aware of the local context and local cultural aspects that can create misunderstandings in the relationship with the students, particularly the ones from a Muslim background.

Section 7: Partnership

Principle 21: Partnership is necessary among all those involved in refugee ministry.

Partnerships are taking place in the refugee ministry with different groups. CIU and USC are the ones providing most of the volunteers, while LSC provides contact with the refugee families that need to be engaged by the church.

Principle 22: For a partnership to function effectively, we recognize that each partner brings meaningful perspective and gifts to the process.

Our partners are bringing meaningful perspectives and gifts to the process. To have Arabic-speaking people among the volunteers is particularly significant, as well as having teachers with training in TESOL and TEFL. Beyond that, to have volunteers with work experience in the Muslim world is extremely helpful.

Principle 23: Partnerships share work, risk, responsibility, accountability, decision-making, and benefits.

The interviews have provided examples of shared work, risk, responsibility, accountability, decision-making, and benefits concerning the partners. One highlight is the volunteers' willingness to serve the refugees beyond the Sunday activities at the church, providing ESL lessons during the week.

SUMMARY OF THE AREAS THE CHURCH IS DOING WELL

Table 1	
Section 1: Ministry Policy and Practice	4 out of 6 principles
Section 2: The Role of Advocacy	1 out of 3 principles
Section 3: The Role of the Church	2 out of 3 principles
Section 5: The Role of Organizations	4 out of 4 principles
Section 6: Ministry Context	3 out of 3 principles
Section 7: Partnership	3 out of 3 principles

AREAS THE CHURCH NEEDS TO IMPROVE

Section 1: Ministry Policy and Practice

Principle 4: Organizations and churches develop ministry strategies based on sound research and assessment.

The church is basing the work on the expertise of other organizations and experienced partners, which suggests that there is much wisdom being exchanged. However, it was pointed out in the interviews that this is an area that needs improvement. Since most of the outside volunteers are students from CIU and USC, the church can improve its ability to do research and assessment by utilizing the capacities of its own volunteers.

*Principle 5: Organizations engage in effective
and honest communication.*

Mostly, verbal communication has been effective and honest, but limited, since it mainly depends on translation from Arabic to English. Positively, the more quickly the students learn English, the more quickly this obstacle will be overcome. To hasten the process, the church should continue helping refugees progress in their learning experience. The ideal scenario would be to offer ESL classes regularly during the week as well. To focus on the refugees' needs and circumstances leads the ESL learning experience to higher results, as Don Snow asserts, "A successful language learning effort needs to be designed according to the learner and the situation."[12]

Section 2: The Role of Advocacy

*Principle 8: Advocacy on behalf of refugees in the public
square and within the Christian community will be
grace-based, honest, and performed with integrity.*

Advocacy on behalf of refugees is a positive aspect of the ministry. The examples provided in the answers reveal extremely good initiatives that have been carried out by the participants of the refugee ministry, within the Christian community. However, regarding advocacy in the public square, there is a need to grow in this area as the answers suggested. From all the organizations that were mentioned in the twenty-three answers, there was not even one devoted exclusively to advocacy. So, this is an indication that the advocacy work is an area that needs further exploration.

*Principle 9: Advocacy is most effective when done in
collaboration with refugees and other advocacy groups.*

In terms of advocacy, there is a need for more work in collaboration with refugees and other advocacy groups. One way for the church

12. Snow, *From Language Learner to Language Teacher*, 9.

to learn more about how to do advocacy involving refugees would be to network with advocacy organizations that are based or active in Columbia.

Section 4: The Role of Refugees

Principle 12: Refugees are involved as partners in ministry.

There are good examples of efforts to involve the refugees as partners in the ministry, but more initiatives in this area can be taken. As the refugees show progress in their resettlement experience, the church needs to continue to explore new ways the refugees can partner in the work and even train them to serve the broader refugee community in Columbia.

SUMMARY OF THE AREAS THE CHURCH NEEDS TO IMPROVE

Table 2	
Section 1: Ministry Policy and Practice	2 out of 6 principles
Section 2: The Role of Advocacy	2 out of 3 principles
Section 4: The Role of Refugees	1 out of 1 principle

There are numerous areas to celebrate concerning the work AHPC is doing, especially as we see the refugees progressing in their resettlement process. One area of evident progress is language acquisition. Interviewees pointed out additional items. However, this introspective look has shown also that there are other areas we need to improve in our ministry to serve our international friends better. Fortunately, this research has raised our awareness as a church in these areas. We continue to discuss each of them as we meet for evaluation and planning. For example, in regard to having the refugees partnering in the work, we discussed the possibility of having some refugees teaching an Arabic class to help the volunteers improve their communication with other Arab refugees.

Since the refugee ministry was established, we committed to meet regularly to evaluate the work so that we could continue to improve the services provided by the church. Our aim has always been to address the needs of the refugees and assist them with excellence.

Over time, we noticed that by showing love, integrity, and professionalism in our work, we were able to build a reputation and respect with our refugee friends. As a result, more refugees and volunteers heard about our work and expressed a desire to join us. In this way, we can fulfill the words of Jesus by bringing glory to our Father in heaven: "Let your light shine before others, that they may see your good deeds and glorify your Father in heaven" (Matt 5:16).

DISCUSSION QUESTIONS

1. Why do refugees need help in their resettlement process?
2. Why is self-evaluation in a ministry developed among refugees so important?
3. Of the factors contributing to the migration crisis, which five do you find the most disturbing? Why?
4. What are some of the practical ways that the Arsenal Hill Presbyterian Church is trying to address the needs of the refugees?
5. What are other principles regarding refugee ministry that should be evaluated?

PRAY FOR THE REFUGEES

Pray for the refugees who have already been resettled that they may be used by God to bless many others who are still displaced. Pray that they will set an example of service that will mobilize the local people and impact the lives of other refugees in their new context.

CALL TO ACTION

Watch the free online movie called "The Stranger" by Evangelical Immigration Table and talk to five friends, at least, about ways you can respond together to the needs of immigrants living in your area: https://vimeo.com/97163476.

7

Your Story

Engaging Refugees in Your Community

The Great Commission is not an option to be considered; it is a command to be obeyed.

—HUDSON TAYLOR

Migration is a universal phenomenon. Migrants come from everywhere and are found in the most unlikely contexts. One way or the other, they shape our daily lives, as Matthew Soerens points out. "In the United States, for example, immigrants or their children were responsible for founding 40 percent of Fortune 500 companies, including brands such as Apple, AT&T, Boeing, Disney, General Electric, Google, and McDonald's."[1] As a result, our world is shrinking. As never before, people from different religions, cultures, and languages are having to learn how to interact, get along, and live together. How can a church fulfill God's mission today without considering the existing migration reality in our current societies?

---

1. Soerens and Yang, *Welcoming the Stranger*, 88.

As Christians, when relating to people in increasingly diverse societies, we need to recognize that our God loves people beyond borders. This is done not just by sending individual missionaries across global lines but by transferring entire mission fields. The Almighty has a global redemption plan and is calling men and women universally through Jesus Christ, "For God so loved the world that he gave his one and only Son, that whoever believes in him shall not perish but have eternal life" (John 3:16).

In his immeasurable love and unsearchable grace, God is also calling the migrant, the displaced, and the refugee. He wants to touch, justify, and transform them "freely by his grace through the redemption that came by Christ Jesus" (Rom 3:24).

Because God loves humankind, Christ sends his church to the world to proclaim his good news to all peoples, "Peace be with you! As the Father sent me, I am sending you" (John 20:21). Therefore, as followers of Jesus, we must fulfill our mission. We need to let as many people as possible have access to what Jesus has done for them. In this way, they will find redemption, forgiveness, and grace. "In him we have redemption through his blood, the forgiveness of sins, in accordance with the riches of God's grace" (Eph 1:7).

Let us submit ourselves to Jesus and allow him to conduct our lives as he is, "the head of the body, the church; he is the beginning and the firstborn from among the dead, so that in everything he might have the supremacy" (Col 1:18). If our obedience to God requires sacrifice, let us identify ourselves with Jesus and suffer for a good cause. As Rick Warren asserts, "We have to sacrifice for what Jesus sacrificed."[2]

LOVING REFUGEES

Since God loves all peoples and calls us to love them as well, the church of our generation needs to turn its eyes to refugees and intentionally minister to them as "Good Samaritans" (Luke 10:25–37).

As we build meaningful relationships with refugees and introduce them to our communities of faith, there will probably be

2. Ong, "Why Must We Care for Refugees?," para. 7.

a socio-cultural impact on our congregations. This can represent a positive impact as long as we are willing to adjust ourselves to the Holy Spirit's work in the lives of the new people God is bringing into our fellowship.

The migratory crisis may cause us much discomfort in the form of perplexity, distrust, or fear. But, as Christians, we must remember to keep the Bible as our compass. As we look to the Holy Scriptures as a whole, we find in them a solid basis for showing compassion to the needy: "Give generously to them and do so without a grudging heart; then because of this the LORD your God will bless you in all your work and in everything you put your hand to" (Deut 15:10).

Because Islamic fundamentalism is such a challenge in our contemporary world, interactions with refugees from a Muslim background can prove a stretching experience for some Christians. Hopefully, it may force us to reexamine our own hearts and even reconsider the biblical basis of our Christian worldview.

The Early Church had to face a similar experience when the first gentiles started embracing the Christian faith. Fortunately, after initial opposition, the disciples recognized the work of the Holy Spirit and understood God's plan for the gentiles, "When they heard this, they had no further objections and praised God, saying, 'So then, even to Gentiles God has granted repentance that leads to life'" (Acts 11:18).

Curiously, at first, the Apostle Paul was rejected by the church in Jerusalem due to his past as a persecutor of believers. After he met the LORD, the disciples had a hard time believing that Paul's conversion was genuine, "When he came to Jerusalem, he tried to join the disciples, but they were all afraid of him, not believing that he really was a disciple" (Acts 9:26). The disciples were consumed by fear and decided to reject Paul, maybe because they did not believe that God could change all kinds of people.

The Bible challenges all disciples to be open to the possibility of God calling into his kingdom people one might consider unlikely. Our prejudices shall not fool us. Despite appearance, ethnicity, or origin, in God's sight, people are all the same. We are all transgressors who need to be justified by God's grace, "There is no difference between Jew and Gentile, for all have sinned and fall short of the glory of God, and all are justified freely by his grace through the redemption that came by Christ Jesus" (Rom 3:22–24).

So, we must never underestimate the power, love, and grace of God revealed in the Scriptures. God does not despise anyone who sincerely comes to him: "God is mighty, but despises no one; he is mighty, and firm in his purpose" (Job 36:5).

It is crucial for us to bear in mind that the gospel, the good news that came from heaven through Jesus Crist, is powerful and intended for sinners. It can transform all people, even those who, like Paul, oppose and persecute the Christian faith. Therefore, Jesus did not come to save those who already consider themselves righteous, but people who have messed up: "It is not the healthy who need a doctor, but the sick. I have not come to call the righteous, but sinners" (Mark 2:17).

The gospel is good news for humankind, including our refugee neighbors.

THE GOSPEL BREAKS DOWN WALLS

In Jesus, God tore down the walls that cause division and brought together Jews and gentiles, groups of people who were enemies and separated by hostility, "For he himself is our peace, who has made the two groups one and has destroyed the barrier, the dividing wall of hostility" (Eph 2:14).

As Paul continues to describe the work of Jesus, he explains that in Jesus, Jews and gentiles were not only brought together but also made into one people, becoming members of the same spiritual body: "His purpose was to create in himself one new humanity out of the two, thus making peace, and in one body to reconcile both of them to God through the cross, by which he put to death their hostility" (Eph 2:15–16).

Indeed, God wants to make all of us part of his family regardless of our background. For this reason, at the cross, God has made us all one: "There is neither Jew nor Gentile, neither slave nor free, nor is there male and female, for you are all one in Christ Jesus" (Gal 3:28).

God welcomes all sorts of people into his kingdom and makes them members of the same family. Likewise, he gives us the privilege to help migrants, as well as people from many other backgrounds, to enter.

Regarding our refugee friends, as a consequence of all the hurt they have experienced in life, they will likely need physical, emotional, and spiritual help. The gospel carries good news for this situation as well. They are part of a redemption plan of a great God who loves the broken and gave his only son to become our "righteousness, holiness and redemption" (1 Cor 1:30).

THE BODY OF CHRIST

Diversity is one of the characteristics of the body of Christ. The church is an organism of many members, with different parts, shapes and functions combined and working together, "supported and held together by its ligaments and sinews, grows as God causes it to grow" (Col 2:19).

If the body of Christ is designed to be diverse, why would we be afraid to seek different distinct expressions and incorporate people from distinguished backgrounds into our faith communities?

Let us not fear diversity. Instead, we look eagerly to what God is doing in our days. Truthfully, the refugee crisis represents an excellent opportunity for us to get in touch with the world's unreached, share the good news of hope with them, and integrate them into a family that expresses how God loves the world.

UNPRECEDENTED OPPORTUNITIES

Imagine that about a decade ago, you felt called by God to share the gospel with Afghanis and decided to say yes to the divine voice like Isaiah, "Here am I. Send me!" (Isa 6:8). As a result of this experience, you would likely need to move to Afghanistan, where 99.9 percent of the people are considered to be unreached, and evangelical

Christians represent only 0.03 percent of the population.[3] But, before transitioning to a new country on the other side of the world, you would have to take some important steps toward preparation. If you would preferably serve overseas in partnership with a Christian organization, you would need to follow some prerequisites. Most Christian organizations working cross-culturally ask their people to invest time in biblical, missiological, and anthropological training, which can take a couple of years. Besides that, you would have to make a great life sacrifice, which would involve things like quitting your job, saying goodbye to your family and friends, leaving your homeland, and establishing yourself in a foreign country in Asia. After getting there, you would still have to deal with enormous challenges such as adapting to the new living environment, learning a new language, and building meaningful relationships. Then, you would be able to start sharing the gospel in a country that is among the world's worst persecutors of Christians, according to the World Watch List published annually by Open Doors.[4]

Our world has changed dramatically in the last ten years, and the migration crisis is one of the contributing factors to the changes we have seen. Today, forcibly displaced people are on the move everywhere at unprecedented levels. As a result of this, Afghanis have become one of the largest displaced people in the world, and there is a great possibility that a considerable number of Afghan refugees have established themselves right where you live. Therefore, if you feel God's calling to the Afghan people today, you have at least two possibilities to consider when contemplating where to develop your ministry geographically. You can still leave the country and go to Afghanistan—where the population needs to hear the gospel—or you can stay and work with Afghan people where you are, according to how God leads you.

The Afghan refugees living in your midst have experienced displacement and resettlement. Hence, they were the ones who had to make the great sacrifice of fleeing their homeland, leaving their family and friends, traveling across countries, and adjusting to life

3. See further Joshua Project, "Afghanistan."
4. See further Open Doors USA, "World Watch List."

in your living context. So, if God leads you to work with Afghanis in your own area, then you are left with the easiest part of the process of reaching them with the gospel. It doesn't mean that you would not have to prepare yourself or make sacrifices and face challenges in your work. However, you would be in a much more comfortable position as you are serving from a context of your own homeland.

Today, more than in any other time in history, engaging refugees is a reality that brings new opportunities to the body of Christ to access and reach the unreached by the gospel. As Brian Hébert asserts: "Missions to the diaspora affords opportunities to reach peoples from closed access countries without the necessary approval from foreign governments. Missions through the diaspora mobilize people who have natural connections to closed access countries."[5]

There are significant advantages to reaching a migrant people group living in a context in which we are established and know very well. Ali Mitchell presents some of these advantages:

> "When I think of work with diasporas, I see the amazing opportunity to reach the nations on our own soil, without the ambiguity that comes from unpredictable political change and upheaval. There is no need for visas or international travel. Pastoral care of those involved in the work can be more easily administered by the sending or equipping churches, and funds can be stretched to support those who work full-time among diaspora communities."[6]

The scenario I am describing here reflects a contemporary reality that touches many other people groups, particularly from Muslim nations. The population of displaced Muslims worldwide is massive. As Hébert asserts, once again, "If all diaspora Muslims were to gather in one location, it would be the sixth-largest Muslim country in the world, ranking just ahead of Turkey and Iran."[7]

---

5. See Hébert, "'With' of Diaspora Missiology," loc. 3384.

6. See Mitchell, "Realidades, Desafios e Oportunidade," 101.

7. See Hébert, "Unengaged Through Diaspora Ministry," loc. 4241–46.

The current human displacement offers us unprecedented opportunities for access to people groups that are now present on our soil. This circumstance allows us to reach the world and proclaim the good news to the people that God has purposely brought from far and wide to become our new neighbors.

A SMALL CHURCH IN COLUMBIA

By his grace, God is using a small church in Columbia, South Carolina, to welcome, express love, plant seeds of hope, and provide access to the good news to a people who may not have had the opportunity before in their previous homeland. What characteristics and practical aspects of this ministry can you apply to your own context, as God has brought people near to you as well?

OUTSTANDING CHARACTERISTICS OF THE REFUGEE MINISTRY

The following characteristics of refugee ministry are essential for fruitful engagement because of their coherence with the Scriptures and best practice principles proposed by the Refugee Highway Partnership. These attributes were evident in the work at Arsenal Hill Presbyterian Church and can be foundational for the ministry that you undertake in your local area.

Abundant Love

The Muslim refugees from Syria and Iraq feel they are loved by the church. Love for them has been manifested by the AHPC in different forms, such as respect, admiration, and recognition of their dignity. These forms show their value as people created in God's image. Love has impacted their lives in such a way that some of them feel that they are receiving more love from Christians than from any other community in Columbia.

Indiscriminate Empathy

No signs of discrimination have been shown toward the refugee community. The refugee ministry has been vigilant to create a welcoming environment for the refugees, as the information in the previous chapters shows. One crucial step in this regard was to adopt a Cultural Sensitivity Document (see Appendix 3) in order to help the volunteers be sensitive to essential aspects of the cultures involved in the relationship. The document is available online as a sign-up form, and all volunteers are required to read and sign it before joining ministry activities.[8] The answers from the questionnaire revealed that a significant reason for this is the caution volunteers take not to refer to the students in the ESL program as refugees. Instead, they call them friends, international friends, or students. This is the language used at the church's website as well.[9] In my evaluation, the fact that the AHPC has the vision to be a multi-ethnic church helps the people to accept the cultural differences found among the refugees and to embrace them just as they are.

Robust Engagement

The church members and volunteers are hugely engaged in the work, serving the refugees almost every weekend for periods of two to three months. Even the pastor and his family are directly involved in the work, teaching in the ESL classes. The volunteers do so much because of their robust engagement in the ministry. Interestingly, no one is paid to do the work. The participants voluntarily cover the costs of their expenses concerning all the services they provide to the refugees.

Strategic Partnerships

Since the AHPC is still in the process of rebuilding its community, the church has been able to carry on the work with the refugees in

8. See further Arsenal Hill Presbyterian Church, "Cultural Sensitivity."
9. See further Arsenal Hill Presbyterian Church, "English Classes."

large part because of the partnerships it has established; especially the volunteers from CIU and USC. The interviews have shown that the establishment of partnerships has been a key aspect in the work developed by the church. It has been important not only to recruit volunteers, but also a skilled workforce of teachers for the ESL program. Some of them are students enrolled in the TESOL program at CIU.

Intentional Recruitment

Church members have shown the ability to mobilize volunteers from two of the universities in Columbia. This explains how a church with only thirty-five active members was serving over forty refugees at the time of this research. It further suggests that for a church to establish a refugee ministry, time must be invested in recruiting, especially for small congregations. One of the challenges of recruiting is balancing time invested in recruitment with time spent on the practical work that needs to be done. The reality is that any time spent on recruitment draws people away from the work. This creates a dilemma of how to maximize time, value, and resources, for if we do not invest any time doing recruitment, it means a small group of people will have to do all the work by themselves.

The church highly appreciates the work of the volunteers. One step the refugee ministry has taken to protect volunteers is to respect their school breaks and holidays by not having classes during these events. Also, when volunteers sign up for the work at the church, they have the option to choose the dates they are able to serve. In this way, they can skip some Sundays in order to rest and be strengthened for the other days.

Before a new season (six to nine weeks) starts, there is always a debrief meeting to promote orientation, accountability, evaluation, training, and encouragement among the volunteers. A speaker is usually invited to share knowledge in a specific area of work, which helps to empower the volunteers.

PRACTICAL INITIATIVES USED TO RESPOND TO THE CURRENT REFUGEE CRISIS

Based on the foundation of love, empathy, partnerships, and robust engagement, there are several practical components of refugee ministry that meet the felt needs of refugees and offer opportunities to build relationships. These practical connecting points were used in Columbia and can be probably be applied to any given context as well:

1. Teaching English (ESL)
2. Helping with translation
3. Explaining aspects of the local culture
4. Introducing life in the city
5. Providing transportation
6. Making appointments
7. Tutoring
8. Making connections
9. Offering friendship
10. Presenting the gospel

PRAYER AND EVANGELISM

Prayer and evangelism were not well-explored in the interviews, although they have been preserved as part of the work conducted by AHPC. These two aspects did not receive much focus on this research because we were strictly following the twenty-three principles based on the *Best Practices for Christian Ministry Among Forcibly Displaced People* by the RHP.

I want to highlight that prayer and evangelism are two crucial aspects of Christian ministry. They glorify God and produce vital results. The *Fruitful Practice Research* from Vision 5:9 network has shown that prayer and evangelism are fruitful practices that lead people to faith in Christ.[10]

---

10. See further "Practices Relating to Seekers."

I recommend that any church undertaking refugee ministry should include these two aspects as core to their ministry and consider them in their regular assessment initiatives.

1) Initiatives Related to Prayer

If possible, believers working with refugees need to develop prayer initiatives to pray with them and for them. In general, Muslim refugees accept and appreciate when a Christian prays for them. In my personal experience, I have not yet found a Muslim who refused prayer, though I am aware of other Christians who had a different experience.

When I ask my Muslim friends to share their prayer requests with me, they usually feel free to do it and thank me for the fact that I am willing to pray for them. Whenever it is possible, I pray for them in their presence. Following up, the next time we meet, I ask them if God has answered any of our previous prayers. In the case of an affirmative answer, we then pray to thank God. If I do not receive an affirmative answer, I ask for new prayer requests, and we continue praying. I have also had Muslim friends ask me to share my prayer requests and afterward commit to pray for me. In this way, prayer becomes a mutual part of our relationship.

Corporate prayer is also essential and needs to be encouraged in a refugee ministry. In Columbia, we had three corporate prayer initiatives happening specifically to intercede for the refugees and the work among them. Two of these initiatives were weekly, and one was monthly. The prayer gatherings occurred in home groups and at the church.

A tool that can be used to catalyze prayer specifically for refugees is the *30 Ways to Pray for Refugees*,[11] a free online prayer guide that covers eight areas of needs of people living as refugees. This material was produced by a Christian organization called Christar.

---

11. See further "30 Ways to Pray for Refugees."

2) Initiatives Related to the Proclamation of the Gospel

For churches willing to implement a refugee ministry, training on how to share the gospel cross-culturally is essential for equipping volunteers. Assessment of refugee ministry could specifically include how the gospel is being shared in the relationship with the refugees, how intentional the church is about communicating the gospel to them, and what methods the church is using to proclaim the gospel to refugees. A particular method we are exploring at the moment with our audience is called *Al Massira*.[12] We like this method because it was produced by Arab Christians from North Africa and the Middle East. It uses the chronological Bible storytelling approach, and is accessible in Arabic and many other languages.

Also, another tool we have used to share the gospel with our refugee friends is the *Jesus Film*.[13] It is accessible for free in more than 1500 languages of the world. The *Jesus Film* strategically communicates the gospel to people who have never heard and seeks to make disciples from all nations.

LEARNING IN THE PROCESS

As a church, we have been learning many lessons and growing in different areas in the process of establishing a relevant ministry among our international friends. One of the lessons is that education plays an essential role in refugee ministry. As a consequence, we are continually making efforts to raise the standards of our ESL program and promote our students' educational development. Some of the initiatives we are launching include building an ESL library and organizing training workshops to equip the teachers. We have observed a direct correlation between the diligence with which we provide services to refugees, our reputation, and the perceived benefits in their community. As Jan Edwards indicates,

---

12. See further Al Massira's website at www.almassira.org.
13. See further on the Jesus Film at www.jesusfilm.org.

"Having teachers who approach English teaching cautiously, humbly, and knowledgeably, and not arrogantly, benefits students."[14]

EVALUATION AND ASSESSMENT

Based on my experience working with refugees and conducting research in refugee ministry, I understand that evaluation and assessment are key aspects of maintaining the work's progress. Here are ten reasons evaluation and assessment are important:

1. Give a voice to the participants
2. Stimulate accountability
3. Endorse transparency
4. Deal with reality
5. Examine focus
6. Highlight core values
7. Measure performance,
8. Allow improvements
9. Help with planning
10. Promote encouragement

Hence, I recommend an annual evaluation and assessment of the work for the development of high-quality, ongoing refugee ministry. Although it may require some adjustments, *Best Practices for Christian Ministry Among Forcibly Displaced People* provides an excellent evaluation and assessment framework. Moreover, other similar tools can be used or developed by the participants of a refugee ministry, considering each work and context's particular nature.

A WINDOW OF OPPORTUNITY

The numbers from UNHCR reports point to a significant aspect: more than half of the displaced people in the world come from Muslim nations like Syria, Afghanistan, Somalia, Yemen, and many others where there is no freedom of religion as we have in the West. Nevertheless, they are moving to nations like the United States,

14. Dormer, *Teaching English in Missions*, 52.

for instance, where freedom of religion is a fundamental right. In their countries of refuge, they are granted access to the Christian faith. This has been the case for the majority of the refugees that the AHPC is engaging. Men, women, and children are having access to a church and to the gospel for the first time in their lives. Therefore, this scenario represents an extraordinary missional opportunity.

This research has shown that there are churches around the world feeling compelled by the teachings of the Scriptures and responding biblically to the current refugee crisis. Also, there are best practices that can be learned and applied by Christians who want to develop effective initiatives to serve refugees.

Christians worldwide are being called to action, not only by the demands of the current scenario but also by God. He loves the stranger and commands his people to love them as well. Thus, the global church should make the most of this unprecedented opportunity to share the gospel with precious people whom God loves so much.

WHAT IS YOUR RESPONSE?

The Bible speaks of a God who loves the stranger and has instructed his people, in both Testaments, to reproduce his character and bless the foreigner.

We live in a time of crisis. The number of people forcibly displaced worldwide continues to rise, therefore we must find viable ways to protect individuals who are genuinely living in vulnerable, desperate, and dangerous situations.

The current refugee crisis represents an opportunity for the church to touch the lives of millions of refugees, many of them yet unreached by the gospel, responding biblically to a challenge that is deeply affecting our world today.

The case study based on the refugee ministry developed by the AHPC in Columbia underlines an approach that can be reproduced in many areas within and beyond the United States. This approach's characteristics are abundant love, indiscriminate empathy, robust engagement, strategic partnerships, and intentional recruitment. In addition, this study refers to several practical initiatives that can be undertaken by Christians who are willing to respond to God's call among the refugees.

Our God is using his people to engage the challenges of the current refugee crisis in order to reveal his glory to the millions of individuals who are scattered around the world. Likewise, the Almighty wants to use us individually to respond in obedience to the heavenly calling by extending hospitality, grace, and truth to those who are away from home, helpless, and unprotected. Will you help change these stories?

DISCUSSION QUESTIONS

1. Why do we tend to naturally fear interactions with people who are different? In light of the Scriptures, what can we do about it?
2. What are some of the refugee initiatives happening around you?
3. What are you going to do about the refugee ministry ideas that you found in this study?
4. Who are five people within your sphere of influence that could benefit from the content of this study? Are you willing to share your learning experience with them and others?
5. In what practical ways will you respond to the current refugee crisis? How can we change these stories?

PRAY FOR THE REFUGEES

Pray that during their diaspora experience, refugees will have access to the gospel and meet Jesus. Pray that God will continue to build his church, bringing to faith refugees who represent unreached people groups and have never had the opportunity to hear the gospel.

CALL TO ACTION

Access the "Figures at a Glance" page by UNHCR (www.unhcr.org/figures-at-a-glance.html). Next, make a list of the most significant challenges related to forcibly displaced people. Consider how you could contribute to overcoming these challenges and, then, write a plan explaining how you will address at least one of them.

Appendix 1

Gathering the Stories

METHODOLOGY

Interviews were the main tool in the methodology of this qualitative research. The purpose of the research was to evaluate how well the Arsenal Hill Presbyterian Church was developing its refugee work in order to address the needs of the Syrian, Iraqi, Congolese, and Vietnamese refugees in Columbia.

THE INTERVIEWS

In total, twelve people were interviewed. The interviews covered three groups of people involved in the refugee ministry:

1. Church volunteers (seven people),
2. Refugees (four people),
3. Resettlement agency (one person).

To establish the grounds for comparison and conduct the interviews, I developed a questionnaire with twenty-three questions based on the twenty-three principles found in the document called *Best Practices for Christian Ministry Among Forcibly Displaced People*. It was published by the Refugee Highway Partnership in 2016 to help Christian organizations to develop a refugee ministry with excellence.[1] The RHP is a global partner of the World Evangelical Alliance for serving refugees around the world. It was founded in 2011 to serve as a cooperative network and "is a growing worldwide community of Christians who share a commitment to welcome and serve refugees."[2]

THE QUESTIONNAIRE

During the interviews, distinct questions from the questionnaire were asked to different groups of people, according to the following description:

1. *Church volunteers*: seventeen questions (1, 4, 5, 6, 7, 8, 9, 10, 11, 12, 13, 18, 19, 20, 21, 22, and 23),
2. *Refugees*: two questions (2 and 3),
3. *Resettlement agency*: four questions (14, 15, 16, and 17).

The following details the demographic information on those interviewed:

- **Church interviews**: four men and three women. Seven of them are members of the church and one is a volunteer. Six of them have been serving in the ministry since the beginning.

- **Refugee interviews***:* Among the refugees, I interviewed four women, two from Syria and two from Iraq. I interviewed the women because they attend the ministry activities more than the men. The men's participation lessened as they started getting jobs after their first few months living in the United States. Interviewees were from Damascus, Raqqa, Baghdad, and northern Iraq (Kurdish).

- **Agency interview***:* From the agency, I interviewed one woman.

The interviews were conducted in person, by telephone, and by email. In total, six interviews were conducted in person and six by telephone and email.

---

1. See the questionnaire and the principles for best practices in the Appendix.
2. World Evangelical Alliance, "WEA's Engagement with Refugees," para. 1.

As displayed in the *Best Practices for Christian Ministry Among Forcibly Displaced People* document, the questions and answers of the interviews are organized in the following order:

- Section 1: Ministry Policy and Practice
- Section 2: The Role of Advocacy
- Section 3: The Role of the Church
- Section 4: The Role of Refugees
- Section 5: The Role of Organizations
- Section 6: Ministry Context
- Section 7: Partnership

DATA ANALYSIS

The data collected from the interviews are presented in chapter 5.

Since twelve people were interviewed based on a questionnaire with twenty-three questions, much data was collected. The extent of this work does not allow all the data from the interviews to be presented. Therefore, I am selective regarding all the data shared and have selected two answers to each of the questions that were asked to the following interviewed people:

1. Church volunteers (seven people);
2. Refugees (four people);
3. Resettlement agency (one person).

Regarding the resettlement agency, since only one person was interviewed, I displayed all the answers from that particular person.

The criteria used to select the answers from church volunteers and refugees were broadness, diversity, and details found in the data that were collected during the interviews. All the people who were interviewed had at least one answer selected to be presented in this work.

Appendix 2

The Twenty-three Principles

*Based on the Best Practices for Christian Ministry
Among Forcibly Displaced People and
the Twenty-three Questions Developed for the
Interviews*

The twenty-three principles developed by the Refugee Highway Partnership[1] were the basis for the pertinent questions I developed to use in interviews:

SECTION 1: MINISTRY POLICY AND PRACTICE

- **Principle 1:** Effective refugee ministry has relationship with God and people at its core.

- **Question 1:** Regarding the people involved in the refugee ministry, what are the signs of their relationship with God and other people?

- **Principle 2:** Refugees receive affirmation of their dignity, value, and the contribution they make.

1. Used with permission granted by the Refugee Highway Partnership.

- **Question 2:** Do you feel affirmed by the church in your dignity and value?

- **Principle 3:** Organizations and churches assist refugees in response to their needs without discrimination.

- **Question 3:** Is the church assisting you in response to your needs without discrimination?

- **Principle 4:** Organizations and churches develop ministry strategies based on sound research and assessment.

- **Question 4:** Are you developing your ministry strategies based on sound research and assessment? If not, on what are you basing your ministry strategies?

- **Principle 5:** Organizations engage in effective and honest communication.

- **Question 5:** How effective and honest do you think your communication with the refugees is?

- **Principle 6:** Effective refugee ministries are learning entities.

- **Question 6:** Do you see your group (people involved in the refugee ministry) as a learning entity?

SECTION 2: THE ROLE OF ADVOCACY

- **Principle 7:** The motivation for advocacy is for the benefit of those represented.

- **Question 7:** How motivated are you for advocacy on behalf of the refugees?

- **Principle 8:** Advocacy on behalf of refugees in the public square and within the Christian community will be grace-based, honest, and performed with integrity.

- **Question 8:** How do you do advocacy on behalf of the refugees in the public square and within the Christian community? Is it grace-based, honest, and performed with integrity?

- **Principle 9:** Advocacy is most effective when done in collaboration with refugees and other advocacy groups.

- **Question 9:** Are you working in collaboration with refugees and other advocacy groups?

SECTION 3: THE ROLE OF THE CHURCH

- **Principle 10:** The local church plays a vital role in ministry to refugees.

- **Question 10:** What is the role of the church concerning the refugee ministry?

- **Principle 11:** Local churches will utilize appropriate external resources for effective refugee ministry.

- **Question 11:** What are the external resources the church is utilizing in the refugee ministry?

SECTION 4: THE ROLE OF REFUGEES

- **Principle 12:** Refugees are involved as partners in ministry.

- **Question 12:** Are the refugees involved as partners in the ministry? How?

- **Principle 13:** Agencies are assisting refugee churches in accomplishing their vision and mission.

- **Question 13:** What are the agencies that are assisting the church in accomplishing the vision and mission of the refugee ministry?

SECTION 5: THE ROLE OF ORGANIZATIONS

- **Principle 14:** Agencies are empowering local host country churches in refugee ministry.

- **Question 14:** How are you empowering local churches in refugee ministry?

- **Principle 15:** Agencies utilize resources beyond their own and are cooperating with other groups.

- **Question 15:** Is your agency utilizing resources beyond your own and cooperating with other groups?

- **Principle 16:** Agencies are networking with other ministries along the "highway."

- **Question 16:** How is your agency networking with other ministries along the "highway"?

- **Principle 17:** Agencies seek to resource their ministries from host country economies.

- **Question 17:** Is your agency seeking to resource your ministries from your host country's economy?

SECTION 6: MINISTRY CONTEXT

- **Principle 18:** Refugee organizations collaborate appropriately with the church, giving careful consideration to the regional, cultural, political, and historical context.

- **Question 18:** Is any organization collaborating appropriately with the church, giving careful consideration to the regional, cultural, political, and historical context? How is it happening?

- **Principle 19:** Ministries are flexible, innovative, and creative in responding to changing conditions along the Refugee Highway.

- **Question 19:** Is the ministry flexible, innovative, and creative in responding to changing conditions along the Refugee Highway?

- **Principle 20:** The local context will be understood in order to inform and influence all ministry activity.

- **Question 20:** How well do you understand your local context? Are you aware of potential risks and crises in your specific ministry context?

SECTION 7: PARTNERSHIP

- **Principle 21:** Partnership is necessary among all those involved in refugee ministry.

- **Question 21:** Are partnerships happening in your refugee ministry? With whom? In which areas?

- **Principle 22:** For a partnership to function effectively, we recognize that each partner brings meaningful perspective and gifts to the process.

- **Question 22:** What are the meaningful perspectives and gifts your partners are bringing to the process?

- **Principle 23:** Partnerships share work, risk, responsibility, accountability, decision-making, and benefits.

- **Question 23:** What are some of the examples of shared work, risk, responsibility, accountability, decision-making, and benefits concerning your partners?

Appendix 3

Cultural Sensitivity Document

BY ALI MITCHELL

When our international friends enter our culture and society, they are beginning a journey with many unknowns. They may expect our culture, even of people who call ourselves Christians, to closely mirror what is shown in TV shows, movies, gaming, etc. We have an opportunity to demonstrate how our biblical beliefs, more than our culture, govern how we live our lives.

Culture goes the other way too. When we befriend people from other cultural backgrounds, we are embarking on a journey into new territory, entering into people's lives who have very different ways of doing things.

Understanding and being sensitive to the cultures and customs of our international friends is hugely important for welcoming them well, for building trust with them, and for glorifying the lord in how we relate to them.

The purpose of this document is to help to equip all our volunteers with knowledge and awareness for this cultural journey into the lives of our friends, especially the Syrian families we have come to know and love through our ESL program. In presenting this knowledge, we draw on the Lord's gracious provision of long experience in the Muslim world and among Muslims and other cultural groups here in America.

THE HONOR AND SHAME WORLDVIEW

All the aspects of the cultural expression included here fall within a very important paradigm in most Eastern cultures: the honor/shame worldview paradigm. Mastering the proper ways of interaction can show honor instead of shame, both in terms of Muslim people we meet and our own reputation. Of course, some of the Muslims we meet may already be making big adjustments to our Western cultural context, but if we emphasize an awareness of the things listed below, we will be much less likely to offend our Muslim friends and much more likely to honor them and their families.

THE IMPORTANCE OF FAMILY AND COMMUNITY

We may be very used to our individualistic Western culture. Still, for Muslim people, an individual finds his or her identity, honor, respect, meaning, and so much more, as a member of a family and community. It is so important for us to remember this when relating to individual Muslims, and to try to understand the implications of our words and actions, not just for the one person we are talking to, but for his or her family and cultural or religious group. The actions of the individual person impact a family or community's honor significantly.

VERBAL GREETINGS

What do you answer when someone says to you, "What's up?" "Not much," right? The words don't seem to have any meaning beyond acknowledging that there is another human being somewhere near us. The opposite thing happens routinely in many Muslim cultures. People can take quite a long time greeting each other because after they ask about the person him or herself, they go on to ask about the person's family and health and other aspects of their life from different angles. The Islamic greeting, *Assalam-o-Aleykum!* (Peace be upon you!), and its reply, *Wa Aleykum Assalam!* (And upon you peace!), is the appropriate way to greet Muslims the world over, even in places where greetings are still used since pre-Islamic times.

SHAKING HANDS

Always use the right hand. As a rule, men and women should not shake hands. Some Muslims will place their hand over their heart after shaking hands, like in Pakistan and Afghanistan. In some cultures, it is important to greet everyone in a room when entering the room, which can include shaking hands.

BEYOND SHAKING HANDS

Muslims will often hug members of the same sex on special occasions (as in *Eid* celebrations) or if old friends have not seen one another for a long time. Some Arabs will "air kiss" next to one another's faces, but only among the same gender.

CONTACT BETWEEN MEN AND WOMEN, BOYS AND GIRLS

It is best to avoid all contact with people of the opposite sex. Some Western women find it very natural to touch a man's arm when talking to him, but this should definitely be avoided. Normal and perfectly acceptable ways of relating within Western cultures can communicate very unintended things to Muslims. Muslims can interpret eye contact, smiling, laughter, spending time together, and any kind of physical touch between men and women as an indication of affection beyond mere friendship. It is important for men to minister only to men and for women to minister only to women.

LAUGHTER

Humor and laughter are a great part of relationships. At the same time, it is better to be conservative in how we relate to people of the opposite sex in the area of laughter, as mentioned above. In some Muslim cultures, too much familiarity between men and women in laughter can appear scandalous.

EYE CONTACT AND WINKING

It is always best to avoid or minimize eye contact between men and women. This may be especially difficult for Western people who are used to a more direct interaction with people around them, but it is important to remember, as direct eye contact can be interpreted as being very forward. Avoid winking, as in some Muslim cultures winking has sexual connotations.

USE OF THE RIGHT HAND ONLY

Never use your left hand for shaking hands, eating, drinking, pointing at anything, or handing something to someone. The left hand is associated with bodily functions below the waist, usually used when going to the bathroom.

GESTURING

The safest way to gesture at someone or something is to use the entire hand. The way we point to or at something or someone in Western culture may appear very rude in Muslim cultures. Pointing with one finger, using the thumbs-up sign, the "ok" sign, and beckoning for someone to come using an upturned hand are offensive in many Muslim cultures. When beckoning someone to come to you, it is best to use a downturned palm.

FEET

The soles of the feet are considered dirty by many Muslim cultures. Hence, it is good to avoid crossing one's legs so that the bottom of one's feet is facing someone else in the room. Another thing to remember is that if you ever have an opportunity to visit a mosque, it is good to sit on the floor with legs crossed and your feet under you, avoiding the more comfortable position of leaning against the back wall with your legs straight out.

SHOES

Muslims remove their shoes when entering a mosque and typically a home. This is good to remember when visiting the homes of our Syrian friends.

PORK

Pork is so taboo for Muslims that for some more secularized Muslims not eating pork defines what it means to be a Muslim. Needless to say, avoiding pork or references to pork around Muslims is helpful. What do you do when a Muslim asks you if you eat pork or asks you what it tastes like? One suggestion is to talk about what Jesus said in Matthew 15:10-20. He says, "It is not what goes into the mouth that defiles a person, but what comes out of the mouth." Focusing on the words of Jesus and even reading the passage with a Muslim person may not seem to disarm the immediate question, but it may give them an opportunity to think more deeply about the real importance of their question. Peter's experience with adjusting to God's grace for the gentiles in Acts 10 is another good place to end up with Muslims.

ALCOHOL

Despite the strict prohibition against drinking alcohol in Islam, many Muslims do drink, some more discretely than others. For example, Pakistan is facing a growing problem with alcoholism and deaths related to home-brewed alcoholic drinks. However, Muslims universally acknowledge that Islam forbids drinking alcohol, so we should avoid using alcohol around Muslims or joking about it.

CLOTHING

Women will feel more comfortable around Muslims if they dress more conservatively. What does this mean? A longer-length dress or skirt is fine. Stay away from sleeveless shirts. Shorts must be avoided entirely. If wearing pants, which is ok, a longer shirt covering the body is acceptable. If visiting a mosque, it is best to be prepared with a headscarf, which some mosques even require for women visitors. Likewise, men will communicate respect for Muslims if they dress conservatively. Even though some Muslims may appear more informal, it is still better to dress wearing casual slacks and a decent shirt, especially when first meeting people. Muslims do wear jeans, but many times will dress a little nicer when going out. In many Muslim countries, men are often careful to cover themselves, even wearing long sleeves. Shorts should be avoided by men as well, except when taking part in sports events or when with very close Muslim friends.

DEMEANOR

It is impossible to overestimate the positive impact of a cheerful and friendly demeanor in our relationships with Muslims. Some Christians have become overwhelmingly loved and accepted within Muslim cultures through consistently demonstrating a friendly, warm, smiling attitude toward others, even earning the descriptor "very good human being." We cannot overstate the benefit and blessings that come from a healthy emphasis on being the "fragrance of Christ" among our Muslim friends.

EVENTS AND PEOPLE VERSUS TIME

Although many Muslims do appreciate how punctual we tend to be in the West, many Muslim cultures do default to placing a high value on the event and the person over punctuality. This issue requires patience for those used to people arriving on time and events starting at the stated time. Being impatient will achieve nothing good.

In the Western context, Muslims may well be much more punctual than in some Muslim cultures. However, if we emphasize giving attention to people and a willingness to spend time with them, we can't go wrong. People from many other cultures view Westerners, including Americans, as enslaved to our schedules and calendars. Muslims can be pleasantly surprised when we love them through an "unrushed" demonstration of attentiveness and friendship. This is just one more way to show them honor and respect.

INVITATIONS

Many Muslims will greatly appreciate being given a printed invitation to an event. This is especially true of Iranians and of others as well.

HOSPITALITY

It has been said that it is hard to outdo Muslims when it comes to hospitality. Most Muslim cultures have hospitality firmly built into them. This characteristic is partly due to the emphasis on earning merit in Islam by showing hospitality to guests. Some of this also comes from the desert hospitality of the Middle East, where a person's own honor is at stake based on their ability to welcome and protect guests and even enemies. No matter the motivation, Muslim hosts are some of the most gracious, generous, and self-sacrificing of any peoples. We would do well to receive their hospitality graciously and show them extravagant hospitality as well. One part of showing hospitality is serving food or drinks to guests without asking, as, in some cultures, they may politely refuse one or more times. Another part is showing how much we care by finding out what foods are acceptable to them (*halal*) and which are forbidden (*haram*).

GIFT-GIVING

Muslim cultures vary on whether it is appropriate for a guest to bring a gift when invited to a Muslim person or family's home.

There are resources online that can answer this question specific to the person's culture, giving the invitation.

HOLY BOOKS

Placing the Qur'an on the floor or even on a chair where someone would sit is considered a sign of great disrespect to the holy book. We should show respect for all holy books, including the Qur'an and the Bible. Biblical references, Bibles and New Testaments, and devotional materials should not be kept in or displayed in bathrooms, which are considered an inappropriate environment for holy books. Bibles should be placed respectfully on a table or shelf when hosting Muslims at a Christian venue or in a Christian home. To give an idea of how seriously Muslims take respect for their holy book, Muslim homes will often feature a special shelf up high in the room, especially for holding the Qur'an. So, when carrying the Bible, we should hold it with our right hand, at least above waist level.

RESPECT FOR OLDER PEOPLE

This is an area of great opportunity for us in building relationships with Muslims. Older people receive great respect in many Muslim cultures, though this beautiful and biblical aspect of culture is being lost, even in some of the most traditional societies. We may show respect for older Muslim people we meet by using terms like Doctor, Mr., or Mrs., for example, or by letting them walk in front of us or go through a door ahead of us. Serving them first when it comes to food or drinks goes a long way in building goodwill and relationships of trust.

HONOR AND RESPECT

If Muslim people know that you are trying to show them honor and respect, they will more easily forgive any cultural blunders you may make. How can you do this? Being agreeable when talking with those older than you, rather than disagreeing with them or arguing with them, is one very powerful way. Deferring to those in authority and being aware of people's status within their own community or culture is another. Learning about a Muslim immigrant's culture, customs, traditions, religion, history, and geography of their country also does wonders for relationships with Muslim people, who are often surprised to find out that we know anything at all about such things. Yes, there is a robust patriarchal honor system in many Muslim cultures that has evil tendencies, such as honor killing of apostates from Islam or of girls who date or marry outside of their family's wishes. We do not want to show respect for this broken and godless aspect of some Muslim cultures. However, we wish to emphasize the fact that so many of the things listed above for appropriate interaction with Muslims and avoiding offense are in fact ways of showing honor and respect, in keeping with the biblical commands to regard others as more important than ourselves and to do to others as we would have them do to us, "Do nothing out of selfish ambition or vain conceit. Rather, in humility value others above yourselves, not looking to your own interests but each of you to the interests of the others. In your relationships with one another, have the same mindset as Christ Jesus" (Phil 2:3–5).

Ali Mitchell *served in Pakistan from 1993 to 2001 and is currently welcoming refugees and other newcomers to the United States, including many from the Muslim world. Ali is the coordinator of the Refugee Program at the Arsenal Hill Presbyterian Church in Columbia, South Carolina.*

Appendix 4

Ten Organizations Dedicated to Helping Refugees

UNITED NATIONS HIGH COMMISSIONER FOR REFUGEES

www.unhcr.org

UNHCR, the United Nations Refugee Agency, is a global organization dedicated to saving lives, protecting rights and building a better future for refugees, forcibly displaced communities and stateless people.

REFUGEE HIGHWAY PARTNERSHIP

www.refugeehighway.net

The World Evangelical Alliance has a longstanding commitment to welcoming and assisting refugees, now significantly strengthened through the work of the Refugee Highway Partnership and the WEA Refugee Task Force.

WORLD RELIEF

www.worldrelief.org

World Relief is an international relief and development agency. World Relief provides different kinds of support to victims of poverty, disease, hunger, war, disasters, and persecution.

SAMARITAN'S PURSE

www.samaritanspurse.org

Samaritan's Purse is an evangelical Christian humanitarian aid organization that provides aid to people in physical need as a key part of Christian missionary work.

INTERNATIONAL ASSOCIATION FOR REFUGEES

www.iafr.org

IAFR is an international Christian nonprofit agency devoted to the mission of helping people survive and recover from forcibly displacement. Together with the church, it is a force for hope, healing, and recovery in the world.

INTERNATIONAL RESCUE COMMITTEE

www.rescue.org

The International Rescue Committee is a global humanitarian aid, relief, and development nongovernmental organization. It responds to the world's worst humanitarian crises, helping to restore health, safety, education, economic wellbeing, and power to people devastated by conflict and disaster.

REFUGEES INTERNATIONAL

www.refugeesinternational.org

Refugees International (RI) advocates for lifesaving assistance and protection for displaced people and promotes solutions to displacement crises.

MERCY CORPS

www.mercycorps.org

Mercy Corps is a global humanitarian aid agency engaged in transitional environments that have experienced some sort of shock: natural disaster, economic collapse, or conflict.

DOCTORS WITHOUT BORDERS

www.doctorswithoutborders.org

Doctors Without Borders/Médecins Sans Frontières (MSF) help people worldwide where the need is greatest, delivering emergency medical aid to people affected by conflict, epidemics, disasters, or exclusion from health care.

NEXTMOVE

www.nextmove.net

NextMove is a ministry sponsored by Frontier Ventures (formerly known as the US Center for World Mission) and Converge Worldwide with the focus to help mission-sending agencies to effectively engage in diaspora missions, both globally and in North America. The organization provides resources as solutions for diaspora missions.

Bibliography

"30 Ways to Pray for Refugees." www.christar.org/explore/resources/30-ways-pray-refugees.

Abboud, Samer N. *Syria*. Malden: Polity, 2016.

Adeney, Miriam. *Kingdom without Borders: The Untold Story of Global Christianity*. Downers Grove: InterVarsity, 2009.

"Almost Half of Practicing Christian Millennials Say Evangelism Is Wrong." www.barna.com/research/millennials-oppose-evangelism.

Amnesty International. "Facts & Figures: Syria Refugee Crisis & International Resettlement." www.amnesty.org/en/latest/news/2014/12/facts-figures-syria-refugee-crisis-international-resettlement.

———. "What's the Difference Between a Refugee and an Asylum Seeker?" www.amnesty.org.au/refugee-and-an-asylum-seeker-difference.

Anderson, Benedict R. O'G. *Imagined Communities: Reflections on the Origin and Spread of Nationalism*. London: Verso, 2006.

Aquilina, Mike. *The Way of the Fathers: Praying with the Early Christians*. Huntington: Our Sunday Visitor, 2000.

Arlund, Pam. "Opportunities and Threats in the Muslim World." In *Fruit to Harvest: Witness of God's Great Work Among Muslims*, edited by Gene Daniels et al., 876–1055. Pasadena: William Carey Library, 2019. Kindle ed.

Arsenal Hill Presbyterian Church. "Cultural Sensitivity." www.arsenalhill.org/cultural-sensitivity.

———. "English Classes." www.arsenalhill.org/english-classes.

———. "Our Roots." www.arsenalhill.org/our-roots.

Atwan, Abdel Bari. *Islamic State: The Digital Caliphate*. Oakland: University of California Press, 2015.

Atwood, Kylie. "U.S. Hits Refugee Limit for 2017." *CBS News*, July 12, 2017. www.cbsnews.com/news/u-s-hits-refugee-limit-for-2017.

Balouziyeh, John. *Hope and a Future: The Story of Syrian Refugees*. United States: Time, 2016.

Banks, Lesline. *Love Thy Neighbor Because Man a Dust*. Bloomington: AuthorHouse, 2019.

Basilan, Marvie. "Muslim Refugees Converting to Christianity in Berlin Church." *The Christian Post*, October 2, 2020. https://www.christianpost.com/news/muslim-refugees-converting-to-christianity-in-berlin-church.html.

Bauman, Stephan, et al. *Seeking Refuge: On the Shores of the Global Refugee Crisis*. Chicago: Moody, 2016.

Brown, Lee. "3 Human Traffickers Each Jailed 125 Years for Drowning of Refugee Boy." New York Post, March 16, 2020. https://nypost.com/2020/03/16/3-human-traffickers-each-jailed-125-years-for-drowning-of-refugee-boy.

Bruce, F. F. *Acts*. New International Commentary on the New Testament. Grand Rapids: Eerdmans, 1996.

Bukhari, Sahih. *The Collection of Hadith*. Translated by M. Muhsin Khan. Vol. 4, Bk. 55, No. 546. Kingdom of Saudi Arabia: Islamic University, 1991.

Cockerill, Gareth Lee. *The Epistle to the Hebrews*. Grand Rapids: Eerdmans, 2012.

Creswell, John W. *Design: Qualitative, Quantitative, and Mixed Methods Approaches*. Los Angeles: SAGE, 2003.

Daniels, Gene, et al., eds. *Fruit to Harvest: Witness of God's Great Work Among Muslims*. Pasadena: William Carey Library, 2019.

De Oliveira, Jairo. "Syrian Refugees in Columbia: Responding to the Current Refugee Crisis from a Biblical Perspective." MA thesis, Columbia International University, 2016.

"Diaspora Judaism." www.britannica.com/topic/Diaspora-Judaism.

Dimock, Michael, "Defining Generations: Where Millennials End and Generation Z Begins." https://www.pewresearch.org/fact-tank/2019/01/17/where-millennials-end-and-generation-z-begins/.

Diocese of Liverpool. "Refugees—Responding with Heart and Mind." www.liverpool.anglican.org/Refugees-Responding-with-Heart-and-Mind%20.

Dormer, Jan Edwards. *Teaching English in Missions: Effectiveness and Integrity*. Pasadena: William Carey Library, 2011.

Durham, John I. *Word Biblical Commentary*. Vol. 3, *Exodus*. Grand Rapids: Zondervan, 2015.

Edwards, Adrian. "Needs Soar as Number of Syrian Refugees Tops 3 Million." www.unhcr.org/en-us/news/latest/2014/8/53ff76c99/needs-soar-number-syrian-refugees-tops-3-million.html.

Elliston, Edgar J. *Introduction to Missiological Research Design*. Pasadena: William Carey Library, 2011.

"Europe Gets 8,000 Refugees Daily." *BBC*, September 25, 2015. www.bbc.com/news/world-europe-34356758.

European Union. "Questions and Answers on the EU-Turkey Readmission Agreement and Visa Liberalisation Dialogue." http://avrupa.info.tr/uploads/Q-A_EU-Turkey-Readmission-Agreement.doc.

Fiddian-Qasmiyeh, Elena, et al., eds. *The Oxford Handbook of Refugee and Forced Migration Studies*. Oxford Handbooks Series. Oxford: Oxford University Press, 2014.

Gatrell, Peter. *The Making of the Modern Refugee*. Oxford: Oxford University Press, 2013.

George, Sam, and Marie Adeney, eds. *Refugee Diaspora: Missions Amid the Greatest Humanitarian Crisis of the World*. Pasadena: William Carey Library, 2018. Kindle ed.

Goodwin-Gill, Guy S., and Jane McAdam. *The Refugee in International Law*. Oxford: Oxford, 2007.

Graham, Billy, and Ruth Graham. *The Faithful Christian: An Anthology of Billy Graham*. New York: McCracken, 1994.

Green, Joel B, ed. *Dictionary of Scripture and Ethics*. Grand Rapids: Baker Academic, 2011.

Greve, Joan E. "Refugees in America: By the Numbers." *Washington Week*, January 30, 2017. https://www.pbs.org/weta/washingtonweek/blog-post/refugees-america-numbers.

Guthrie, Stan. *Missions in the Third Millennium: 21 Key Trends for the Twenty-First Century*. Waynesboro: Paternoster, 2000.

Hébert, Brian. "Respondendo ao Fenômeno da Imigração." In *Refugiados, Peregrinos e Forasteiros*, edited by Jairo de Oliveira, 105–16. Londrina: Descoberta, 2017.

———. "The Unengaged Through Diaspora Ministry." In *Fruit to Harvest: Witness of God's Great Work Among Muslims*, edited by Gene Daniels et al., 4226–365. Pasadena: William Carey Library, 2019. Kindle ed.

Hébert, Jacques. "The 'With' of Diaspora Missiology: The Impact of Kinship, Honor, and Hospitality on the Future of Missionary Training, Sending, and Partnership." In *Diaspora Missiology: Reflections on Reaching the Scattered Peoples of the World*, edited by Michael Pocock and Enoch Wan, 3375–654. EMS series 23. Pasadena, CA: Carey, 2015. Kindle ed.

Houston, Fleur S. *You Shall Love the Stranger as Yourself: The Bible, Refugees, and Asylum*. New York: Routledge, 2015.

Human Rights Watch. "Syria: Events of 2016." https://www.hrw.org/world-report/2017/country-chapters/syria.

Im, Chandler H., and Tereso C. Casiño. "Introduction." In *Global Diasporas and Mission*, edited by Chandler H. Im and Amos Yong, 1–16. Oxford: Regnum, 2014.

International Association for Refugees. "Terminology of Forced Displacement." https://global-uploads.webflow.com/5e753e90e64659ba51ecd6ad/5eaad3384c1f30868bdf40d6_Terminology%20of%20Forced%20Displacement%20v201906%20US%20Letter.pdf.

International Crisis Group. "What's Driving the Global Refugee Crisis?" www.crisisgroup.org/global/what-s-driving-global-refugee-crisis.

International Organization for Migration. "Key Migration Terms." www.iom.int/key-migration-terms.

―――. "Mediterranean Migrant Arrivals Reach 4,485 in 2018; Deaths Reach 201." www.iom.int/news/mediterranean-migrant-arrivals-reach-4485-2018 -deaths-reach-201.

―――. "United Nations High Commissioner for Refugees." http://cb4ibm. iom.int/bmc/index.php?option=com_content&view=article&id=65&Ite mid=60.

Jacobsen, Douglas. *Global Gospel: An Introduction to Christianity on Five Continents.* Grand Rapids: Baker Academic, 2015.

John Paul II, Pope. "Speech of the Holy Father John Paul II: Visit to the Refugee Camp of Dheisheh." https://w2.vatican.va/content/john-paul-ii/en/speeches /2000/jan-mar/documents/hf_jp-ii_spe_20000322_deheisheh-refugees. pdf.

Johnstone, Patrick and Dean Merrill. *Serving God in a Migrant Crisis: Ministry to People on the Move.* Colorado Spring: Malcolm Down, 2016.

Jones, Reece. *Violent Borders: Refugees and the Right to Move.* London: Verso, 2016.

Joshua Project. "Afghanistan." https://joshuaproject.net/countries/AF.

Keathley, Hampton J., III. *ABCs for Christian Growth: Laying the Foundation.* Vancouver: Biblical Studies, 2002.

Keller, Timothy. *Generous Justice: How God's Grace Makes Us Just.* New York: Riverhead, 2012.

"Key Terms About the Refugee Crisis, Explained." www.benjerry.com/whats-new/2017/02/refugee-crisis-explained.

Kosern, Khalid. *International Migration: A Very Short Introduction.* Oxford: Oxford University Press, 2007.

Krogstad, Jens Manuel. "Key Facts About Refugees to the U.S." *Fact Tank,* October 7, 2019. www.pewresearch.org/fact-tank/2017/01/30/key-facts-about-refugees-to-the-u-s.

Kurdi, Tima. *The Boy on the Beach: My Family's Escape from Syria and Our Hope for a New Home.* New York: Simon & Schuster, 2018.

The Lausanne Movement. "The Seoul Declaration on Diaspora Missiology." www.lausanne.org/content/statement/the-seoul-declaration-on-diaspora-missiology.

Lutheran Services Carolinas. "Refugee and Immigrant Services." https:// lscarolinas.net/refugee-and-immigrant-services.

Mandryk. Jason. *Operation World: The Definitive Prayer Guide to Every Nation.* Downers Grove: InterVarsity, 2011.

Marshall, I. Howard. *Acts.* Downers Grove: InterVarsity, 2014.

McKinney, Roger. "Eleven Syrian Refugees Now Call Columbia Home." *Columbia Tribune,* September 3, 2016. www.columbiatribune.com/8ff beb60-47f6-5aa8-827c-23023e3a771c.html.

Mitchell, Ali. "Realidades, Desafios e Oportunidade no Trabalho com Diásporas." In *Refugiados, Peregrinos e Forasteiros,* edited by Jairo de Oliveira, 93–104. Londrina: Descoberta, 2017.

Morgan, Timothy C. "1,180 Churches Help World Relief Resettle Refugees at Record Rate." *Christianity Today*, October 20, 2016. www.christianitytoday. com/news/2016/october/1180-churches-world-relief-resettle-refugees-record-rate.html.

Neill, Stephen. *A History of Christian Missions*. London: Penguin, 1991.

Ong, Czarina. "Why Must We Care for Refugees? Because God Commands It, Says Rick Warren." *Christianity Today*, Jaunary 25, 2016. www. christiantoday.com/article/why-must-we-care-for-refugees-because-god-commands-it-says-rick-warren/77615.htm.

Open Doors USA. "World Watch List." www.opendoorsusa.org/christian-persecution/world-watch-list/.

Payne, J. D. *Strangers Next Door: Immigration, Migration and Mission*. Downers Grove: InterVarsity, 2012.

Phillips, Christopher. *The Battle for Syria: International Rivalry in the New Middle East*. New Haven: Yale University Press, 2016.

Pierce, Jonah. *Anissa of Syria: A Christian Refugee's Saga from the Syrian War to the American Dream*. N.p.: CreateSpace, 2015.

Piper, John. *The Supremacy of God in Preaching*. Grand Rapids: Baker, 2015.

Polak, Monique. *The Middle of Everywhere*. Victoria: Orca, 2009.

"Practices Relating to Seekers." www.fruitfulpractice.org/?page_id=613.

Rabil, Robert G. *The Syrian Refugee Crisis in Lebanon: The Double Tragedy of Refugees and Impacted Host Communities*. Lanham: Lexington, 2016.

Refugee Processing Center. "Interactive Reporting." http://ireports.wrapsnet. org/Interactive-Reporting/EnumType/Report?ItemPath=/rpt_WebArrivalsReports/MX%20-%20Arrivals%20by%20Nationality%20and%20Religion.

Refugees Northwest. "By the Numbers: Our Resettled Refugee Neighbors Make a Positive Difference." https://refugeesnw.org/by-the-numbers.

Reliefweb. "UNHCR Jordan Factsheet, May 2019." https://reliefweb.int/report/jordan/unhcr-jordan-factsheet-may-2019.

RHP. "Best Practices for Christian Ministry Among Forcibly Displaced People." www.refugeehighway.net/uploads/5/4/1/8/54189183/refugee_ministry_best_practices_2016.pdf.

Scott, Brantley. "Migration & Diaspora: God's Movement to Reach More People." *EMQ* 53.3 (July 2017) 66–70.

Shakir, M. H. *The Quran*. Elmhurst: Tahrike Tarsile Qur'an, 1985.

Sherfinski, David. "Terrorism Most Important Problem Facing U.S., Americans Say: Poll." *The Washington Times*, December 14, 2015. www. washingtontimes.com/news/2015/dec/14/terrorism-most-important-problem-facing-us-america.

Sherwood, Harriet, and Philip Oltermann. "European Churches Say Growing Flock of Muslim Refugees are Converting." *The Guardian*, June 5, 2016. https://www.theguardian.com/world/2016/jun/05/european-churches-growing-flock-muslim-refugees-converting-christianity.

Sielaff, Victoria. "Our Hospitality Mandate: What Does an Authentic Reception of Syrian Refugees to the United States Look Like?" *EMQ* 53.3 (July 2017) 55–61.

Smither, Edward L. *Christian Martyrdom: A Brief History with Reflections for Today*. Eugene, OR: Cascade, 2020.

———. "Um Olhar Histórico sobre Diásporas." In *Refugiados, Peregrinos e Forasteiros*, edited by Jairo de Oliveira, 31–42. Londrina: Descoberta, 2017.

Smrcek, Helena. *Kingdom Beyond Borders: Finding Hope along the Refugee Highway*. Bloomington: West Bow, 2011.

Snow, Don. *From Language Learner to Language Teacher: An Introduction to Teaching English as a Foreign Language*. Alexandria: TESOL, 2007.

Soerens, Matthew, and Jenny Hwang Yang. *Welcoming the Stranger: Justice, Compassion & Truth in the Immigration Debate*. Downers Grove: InterVarsity, 2010.

Stevenson, Angus. *Oxford Dictionary of English*. New York: Oxford University Press, 2010.

Stott, John R.W. *Basic Christianity*. Downers Grove: InterVarsity, 2009.

Sunquist, Scott W. *Understanding Christian Mission: Participation in Suffering and Glory*. Grand Rapids: Baker, 2013.

Thompson, Brenda. "Old Testament, Principles on Reaching the Refugee." *International Journal of Frontier Missiology* 2.4 (October 1985) 363–68.

Tira, Sadiri Joy, and Tetsunao Yamamori. *Scattered and Gathered: A Global Compendium of Diaspora Missiology*. Oxford: Regnum, 2016.

UNHCR. "Child and Youth Protection." www.unhcr.org/en-us/child-and-youth-protection.html.

———. "Emergency Relief Efforts." www.unrefugees.org/what-we-do/emergency-relief-efforts.

———. "Europe Situation." www.unhcr.org/en-us/europe-emergency.html.

———. "Figures at a Glance." www.unhcr.org/figures-at-a-glance.html.

———. "Frequently Asked Questions about Resettlement." www.unhcr.org/56fa35b16.

———. "Global Report 2019." http://reporting.unhcr.org/sites/default/files/gr2019/pdf/GR2019_English_Full_lowres.pdf.

———. "Global Trends: Forced Displacement in 2016." www.unhcr.org/5943e8a34.pdf.

———. "Global Trends: Forced Displacement in 2018." www.unhcr.org/statistics/unhcrstats/5d08d7ee7/unhcr-global-trends-2018.html.

———. "Internally Displaced People." www.unhcr.org/en-us/internally-displaced-people.html.

———. "Jordan: Zaatari Refugee Camp." http://reporting.unhcr.org/sites/default/files/UNHCR%20Jordan%20Zaatari%20Refugee%20Camp%20Fact%20Sheet%20-%20November%202019.pdf.

———. "Minorities and Indigenous Peoples." www.unhcr.org/en-us/minority-groups.html.

———. "Older People." www.unhcr.org/en-us/older-people.html.

————. "Persons with Disabilities." www.unhcr.org/en-us/people-with-disabilities.html.

————. "Protection." www.unhcr.org/en-us/protection.html.

————. "Resettlement." www.unhcr.org/resettlement.html.

————. "Resettlement and Complementary Pathways." https://data2.unhcr.org/en/documents/download/71062.

————. "Saving Lives at the World's Largest Refugee Camp." www.unhcr.org/news/latest/2019/7/5d2eefd74/saving-lives-worlds-largest-refugee-camp.html.

————. "Shelter." www.unhcr.org/en-us/shelter.html.

————. "Six People Died Each Day Attempting to Cross Mediterranean in 2018–UNHCR Report." www.unhcr.org/news/press/2019/1/5c500c504/six-people-died-day-attempting-cross-mediterranean-2018-unhcr-report.html.

————. "Solutions for Refugees." www.unhcr.org/50a4c17f9.pdf.

————. "This Land is Your Land." www.unhcr.org/en-us/this-land-is-your-land.html.

————. "UNHCR Resettlement Handbook." www.unhcr.org/46f7c0ee2.pdf.

United Nations. "Universal Declaration of Human Rights." www.un.org/en/universal-declaration-human-rights/.

The United Nations News. "Syria: 'Massive Waves of Civilian Displacement and Loss of Life Must Stop Now': UN Special Envoy." https://news.un.org/en/story/2020/02/1056892.

The United States Census Bureau. "Columbia City, South Carolina." www.census.gov/quickfacts/table/PST045216/4516000,45.

The United States Committee for Refugees and Immigrants. "Security Screening of Refugees Admitted to the U.S." https://refugees.org/explore-the-issues/our-work-with-refugees/security-screening.

University of South Carolina. "A Healthy New Start." www.sc.edu/uofsc/posts/2015/12/rajeev_bais_csc.php#.Ws4EOC95C1t.

USA for UNHCR. "What Is a Refugee?" www.unrefugees.org/refugee-facts/what-is-a-refugee/.

Verkuyl, Johannes. *Contemporary Missiology: An Introduction*. Grand Rapids: Eerdmans, 1987.

Vine, William Edwy. *Vines Expository Dictionary of Old Testament Words*. Zeeland: Reformed Church, 2015.

Wan, Enoch. *Diaspora Missiology: Theory, Methodology, and Practice*. Portland, OR: Institute of Diaspora Studies, 2011.

WCCPC World Evangelical Alliance. "Christian Witness in a Multi-Religious World." www.worldevangelicals.org/pdf/1106Christian_Witness_in_a_Multi-Religious_World.pdf.

World Atlas. "The Global Terrorism Index." www.worldatlas.com/articles/the-global-terrorism-index-countries-most-affected-by-terrorist-attacks.html

World Evangelical Alliance. "WEA's Engagement with Refugees." www.worldevangelicals.org/refugees/rhp.htm.

World Relief. "Respond." https://worldrelief.org/respond-2.

Yang, Jenny Hwang. *Immigrants in the USA: A Missional Opportunity.* In *Global Diasporas and Mission.* Oxford, UK: Regnum, 2014.

Yazda and the EAMENA Project. "Yazidi Cultural Destruction Report 2019: Destroying the Soul of the Yazidis: Cultural Heritage Destruction During the Islamic State's Genocide Against the Yazidis." https://354a2745-cd89–499d-8ac2–0340313e364f.filesusr.com/ugd/92f016_b5b37c3356754ba8b30e0f266e5b58d4.pdf.

Scripture Index

SCRIPTURE INDEX

Made in the USA
Columbia, SC
07 December 2020

26563220R00100